Chan—

GIANT
SUCCESS

Keep Climbing !

LEADERSHIP PRINCIPLES AND
BUSINESS STRATEGIES OF

HAL WING
FOUNDER OF
LITTLE GIANT LADDERS

DOUG WING

Quantity sales special discounts are available on quantity purchases by corporations, associations, and others. For details, contact the publisher at the address above.

Orders by U.S. trade bookstores and wholesalers. Email info@BeyondPublishing.net

The Beyond Publishing Speakers Bureau can bring authors to your live event. For more information or to book an event contact the Beyond Publishing Speakers Bureau speak@BeyondPublishing.net

The Author can be reached directly at www.giantsuccess.com

Manufactured and printed in the United States of America distributed globally by BeyondPublishing.net

BEYOND
PUBLISHING

New York | Los Angeles | London | Sydney

ISBN Softcover: 978-1-637922-65-1
ISBN Hardcover: 978-1-637922-69-9

Library of Congress Control Number: 2022902442

FOREWORD
A Family of Tradition and Excellence

Whenever I talk to someone about my Little Giant ladder, they will invariably say, "Oh yeah, I have one of those." The Little Giant Ladder is an iconic ladder and an iconic brand. Legendary. A product that sells for three times the price of their competition because of one word: QUALITY.

It is a product that is clearly best-of-class. Everyone knows it. In fact, you probably have one yourself. What people do not know is that the man behind Little Giant Ladder was the icon.

Hal Wing was the 5' 7" "little giant" behind the Little Giant Ladder. Wing was literally a legend in the building business, a legend in his community and a legend in his church. Oh, not for what he did and what he built, but rather the way he did it, his principal-driven life and for what he gave to others.

His desire for success was fueled by his family and his faith. His drive to innovate and find new ways to sell his product stemmed from his creativity and willingness to bet the farm—literally. His achievement of success was fueled by his passion and perseverance.

His life after achievement was brimming with spontaneous giving and fulfilling his lifelong dream to help people climb their own proverbial ladders. Sometimes, he would come alongside others with his money, sometimes with his help and opportunities and many times with all of the above.

But one of the truly incredible qualities of Hal Wing was his desire to give discreetly rather than build his own reputation. That's how legends do it.

The purpose of this book is to let you see the characteristics of Hal Wing so that you can adopt them and adapt them to your own drive for success.

Read this book carefully as there are lessons on every page. The stories. The quotes. The outcomes. The ideas. The principles. The adventures. The breakthroughs. The spirit. The risks. The rewards. More than a book, Giant Success will provide your guiding light to whatever mountain or ladder you want to climb.

The stories contained inside are unbelievable, yet I promise you they are 100% true. However, the lessons inside the stories are even more powerful than the stories themselves. These are not just his lessons…they are yours.

In keeping with the time-honored Wing tradition of giving, Doug Wing, Hal's faithful son, presents these lessons in a way that you, the reader, can use to build and climb your own ladder.

Giant Success is a book that will guide your way by setting principles to help you and providing instruction to take the actions that will help create your giant success.

> NOTE WELL: Hal Wing did everything full-speed. Running a business, riding a motorcycle or racing a car. Pedal to the metal, often with no brakes.

> NOTE WELL: Hal had a sense of timing that was part of his legend. By eliminating the middleman and going direct-to-consumer through an infomercial, he created

Doug Wing is the true definition of a wingman.
Forty years of actions and deeds prove it.

astronomical success and, at the same time, literally created the infomercial industry.

NOTE WELL: Hal was the pilot and his son Doug was his wingman. Literally and physically.

NOTE WELL: Doug Wing is a person of character and integrity who lives by his word, just like his dad.

– Jeffrey Gitomer

Author of *The Little Red Book of Selling* and *The Little Gold Book of YES Attitude*. Friend and admirer of Doug Wing

My parents and I at their 50th wedding anniversary (2011)

My dad in his suit on his dirt bike in Provo, Utah (early 1980s)

My mother building ladders in American Fork, Utah (late 1970s)

ACKNOWLEDGMENTS

This book has been a labor of love for me. My father, Hal Wing, was an amazing man. I know this because I grew up with him. To hear so many other people share their memories, stories, experiences and love for him with me now, years after his passing, brings me great joy.

I had the pleasure and honor of sitting down with 39 people who agreed to be interviewed for this book. They include family members, friends, employees and business associates of my father. Throughout the process, there was laughter and tears. I heard stories I never knew before and grew to appreciate my dad in a whole new light.

You will hear from each of them as they reflect on the influence my dad had on them and their families. I so appreciate each person who took the time to sit down with me and share their thoughts and feelings about Hal Wing.

The impact my father had on everyone around him was profound. This book is dedicated to him and my mother, Brigitte Mayer Wing. I am so grateful to them for teaching me the value of hard work, integrity, honesty and generosity. I am most thankful to them for giving me a firm foundation in God and in our faith. It set me on the right path so I could live a faithful life.

My mother never sought any of the limelight. I still wonder with amazement how this special lady managed to keep a family of seven children pointed in the right direction when her husband was on the road more than 300 days a year trying to build a ladder company. She never had a driver's license, but somehow, we always had food on the table. She never complained and supported my dad 100% in everything he did. Not only did my mother raise all of us and keep an impeccable home, you also could find her on the shop floor building ladders or in the office doing accounting. Brigitte was my dad's biggest cheerleader and supporter. Without her, Hal Wing would not have been able to become the incredible man that he was.

This book would have never happened without the encouragement of many friends, associates at Little Giant Ladder Systems, and my family. After my dad passed away, so many people told me that his story needed to be shared with the world. Special thanks also go to Jill Walls, Ken Walls and Jeffrey Gitomer for their input, guidance and assistance with this project.

I am incredibly honored to bring this book to you, the reader, and the world. The principles you will learn here are timeless, and the stories are relatable to anyone striving to do better and be better.

I hope this book helps you find your own GIANT success.

– Doug Wing

Hal Wing on the set of QVC (2009)

INTRODUCTION

This is not your typical book about sales and success. It's more than that. It's a book about people. You see, success is based on so much more than intelligence, drive or even experience. It's about who you are as a person and what you can recognize in other people that will make you stand out and rise above.

Hal Wing was a GIANT in the ladder business for sure. But more important than that, Hal was big on people. He valued them, loved them, cared about them and understood them. He created a culture within his organization that made everyone want to achieve more and do their best.

Make no mistake, Hal had high expectations and required 100% effort, but he led by example and took great care to make sure each employee was set up to succeed in their role.

Little Giant Ladders is an American business success story. At the heart of that story is Hal Wing.

In this book, you'll get to know Hal through the stories and experiences of family, friends, employees and colleagues. You'll learn how Hal grew the company from assembling ladders in his carport to becoming the most well-known and sought-after ladder brand ever made.

This book is filled with timeless principles that Hal Wing used to achieve great success. He always said that his gifts, talents and wealth were on loan, and that one day he would be asked what he did with what he was given.

This book is a gift to you from Hal, delivered by me – his son, Doug. As you read this book, adopt these philosophies, practice these principles and implement these strategies, you will not only achieve greatness in your own life and career, but you will be part of the ongoing legacy of the truly remarkable leader, entrepreneur and man, Hal Wing.

Contents

"Patience is a waste of time."

– Hal Wing

Hal Wing's Springville High School
senior yearbook photo (1957)

CHAPTER ONE
Don't Wait for Success, Take It

For many of us, this is the exact opposite of what we've been taught, but it is indicative of the character traits of highly successful people. If you know what you want, go for it, and make things happen. That's what Hal Wing did long before he ever knew anything about ladders.

As a young boy, Hal was always on the move. Despite being told to stay in the yard, the minute his mother's back was turned, off he'd go. Linda McCausland, Hal's cousin, calls it the Wing gene. "No grass will ever grow under Hal's feet," his mother always said.

Hal was a smart kid with a flair for creativity and a true wild side. He taught himself how to play instruments, speak foreign languages, and he even learned to yodel. He had horses and would do tricks on them for the kids in the family. He was non-stop and probably had ADD, though it was never diagnosed.

Hal was a farm kid, so there was always lots of work to be done and no room for laziness. Looking back on Hal's life, it's clear he got many of his success traits from his parents.

Hal's father had a strong work ethic and demanded perfection. Ray Arthur Wing was a foreman on the railroad and in his spare time, he farmed 11 acres. According to Helen Wing Cluff, Hal's sister, their father was a strong and hard-working man who never even went out in the field without getting cleaned up and dressed in clean pressed clothes. The farm was always organized and neat, and the fields were the same. He was a solemn man who never raised his voice or said a swear word, but that didn't mean he did not command respect.

In one instance, Hal had spent a long day working in the field with his dad, and they both were tired. As they approached the house, his father remembered he had not closed a gate on an irrigation ditch. He knew that the neighbor was going to push water through that night and, unless that gate was shut, one of the Wing's fields would be flooded. Hal's father looked at Hal and asked him to go close the gate. Hal unexpectedly replied, "I see your mouth moving, but I can't hear what you're saying." Without a word, Hal's father turned and went to close the gate himself.

Days and weeks went by with no mention of the incident, so Hal thought all was forgotten. A dance was coming up at Hal's school a few weeks later, so Hal went to his dad and asked to reserve the car before any of his other siblings could ask for it. Hal's dad looked him in the eye and calmly said, "I see your mouth moving, but I can't hear what you're saying." Hal walked to the dance that year.

Hal's mother was a perfectionist as well. The house was always tidy with everything in its place, and dishes were never left in the sink overnight. She believed in taking the hand you were dealt and making the best of it. In the Wing house, you never complained, and you never had a bad day. She always told Hal to never give up on what you want. That is something Hal carried with him every day of his life. He later said that he developed his self-belief from his mother, Marguerite Mary Faulkner Wing.

The Wing family also had a strong sense of community. They believed in helping their neighbors and often took fruits and vegetables from their garden to widows and those in the community who needed food. It was their belief that if they had it, they should share it. This became another principle upon which Hal would base his life and career.

As a teenager, Hal suffered with terrible skin trouble and acne. He was often made fun of and taunted at school because of it. It hurt Hal and, some believe, gave him an inferiority complex. But, instead of it keeping him down, Hal used the experience as inspiration to look ahead and focus on what he could control instead of what he couldn't.

In the town where Hal grew up in Utah, there were beautiful mountains. The most expensive houses were nestled on high bluffs, overlooking the town and people below. At about 12 years old, Hal looked up at the mountains above Springville and said to his sister, "Someday I'm going to live on the top of that mountain." And he did.

You see, even at a young age Hal knew what he wanted, and he was willing to work hard and do whatever it took to get there. He didn't wait for someone to teach him things; he taught himself. He didn't let the kids at school make him a victim; he used their bullying as fuel to set and achieve goals for himself.

Everything Hal did was fast. He put his mind to something, and he did it. He rode fast horses, and he had fast motorcycles. Evan Francis, Hal's brother-in-law, first met Hal when he was 13, and in his words, "Hal was a punk." He came riding up on a 1931 Harley Fat Boy and told Evan to get on. Hal went racing through the canyon going over 100 miles an hour with Evan on the back. At the end of the ride, Evan was happy to be alive, and Hal was grinning from ear to ear. "How he got a hold of a Harley at age 13, I still don't know, but when he wanted something, he made it happen, and he wasted no time getting to it."

Hal could never back down from a challenge, and he was never afraid to try something new. Once when out riding snowmobiles with Evan, they came across some kids riding in the same area. One of the kids challenged Hal to a race up a really steep canyon. Hal was in, and off they went. As they climbed, Hal's snowmobile slipped and began to fall. Hal fell all the way down; and the snowmobile landed right behind him in a heap. Without so much as a blink, Hal shrugged it off, jumped on the back of Evan's, and they kept riding. No fall or crash was going to slow Hal down. He just didn't let adversity get in his way...ever.

Hal entered the military after high school and ended up serving in Germany. It is here where he met the love of his life and his wife, Brigitte. One day, while on official military business, Hal saw his future wife as she worked in a local city hall building. Somehow he found out where she lived and knocked on her door. When she opened the door and saw Hal standing there, Brigitte slammed the door in his face. Hal kept showing up at her door, though, until she agreed to go out with him. Ironically, Brigitte's father had told her she was never to marry an American. Enter Hal. As only he could, he won over Brigitte's father, and they married. Hal never gave up on anything he wanted.

Upon returning to the U.S., Hal started his career selling insurance. Because he connected so well with people, he was very good at it and became successful quickly. Brigitte did not know English yet and didn't drive, so Hal made sure she felt comfortable and supported in her new home. The couple settled into life in Utah and had four children.

When tragedy struck Hal's family, Hal and Brigitte took on his deceased brother's three children and adopted them. That meant there were now seven kids at home. Hal was only in his mid-twenties, and he now had a wife and seven kids for whom to provide. While this might seem overwhelming to some, it was fuel in the fire for Hal to do more and be more for his family. Brigitte, too, met each day with grace. As a young mother to seven children, she never complained and kept an impeccable home.

Because Hal was so successful and both he and his wife spoke the language, his company eventually tapped him to open an insurance office in Germany. Hal moved the whole family over, and they spent a few years there.

It was during this time that Hal and Brigitte befriended a German painter who had a primitive prototype for a new kind of ladder. Once he saw that original German ladder, Hal saw his future.

He sat down with Brigitte and told her he wanted to go all-in on the ladder business. With seven kids and a wife to feed and provide for, it would've been easy for Hal to stick to what was safe—focus his attention on his well-paying job and set the ladders aside. Not Hal. He had a vision for what he wanted to accomplish, and he wasn't going to wait until the "perfect time" because there would never be a "perfect time."

Brigitte, who was his biggest fan and supporter, believed in his vision but was hesitant. Making this change meant adjusting to annual earnings of about $8,000, which would not go very far in their family. Brigitte believed in Hal, though, and soon was all-in.

He left the insurance business (and his annual salary which would equate to about $250,000 by today's standards). Hal brought the design back to America and began showing it to family, friends and associates. His excitement and passion for the product helped him pre-sell an entire container of original ladders.

When the ladders arrived, Hal began the process of collecting money and delivering the ladders—only there was a problem. One by one, those commitments to buy became excuses to not buy. Hal was stuck with a bunch of ladders. Instead of complaining or quitting, Hal got to work. He loaded up his car and personally took the ladders on the road, demonstrating them to people every day, week after week until they were all sold. He had a daily quota he had to meet, and he did not stop until he reached it.

One evening, it was getting late and Hal was one ladder short of his goal. His last appointment of the day happened to be with a one-armed man. Determined to make the sale, Hal spent more than an hour with the man, wrestling with the ladder, figuring out how to maneuver it so the man could make good use of it. Success! The man was able to operate the ladder. Hal made the sale and his daily quota.

Over time, Hal and the Germans worked out a licensing agreement which allowed Little Giant Industries to manufacture in the United States. Hal began to innovate and enhance the design on his own. This new ladder had the finest hinges, and there was nothing like it on the market. Hal made his ladder using the best domestically-sourced materials and strong welds. He brought in Doc Shell, who designed the first jigs to build the new ladders and was the very first employee to produce ladders.

The first production facility was located in American Fork, Utah. It was a building infested with both rats and bats. It was so small that inventory had to be moved out in the parking lot so that employees could produce ladders during the day. In the evening, the finished goods that were not shipped that day were brought back into the building and stored for the night.

Little Giant Ladder's first production facility in
American Fork, Utah (late 1970s)

To give you some context, at this time, you could literally go into a Sears store and buy a ladder for $9.99. Little Giant Ladders sold for more than $200. What Hal created was a whole new category of ladders.

While at one of his very first trade shows, Hal had two men come up to him. They were the Werner Brothers, the owners of the largest ladder company in the world at the time (they are still the largest manufacturer of ladders today). They scoffed at Hal and told him he was a fool and that he would surely fail, but that didn't deter Hal. He remembered his mother's words and vowed not to give up because he believed in his product. He was going to make it work. Ironically, the Werner Brothers would go on to try to purchase Little Giant from Hal four times. He never sold to them.

Hal did it all. When he wasn't on the road selling, he would pitch in and help in manufacturing, building ladders and then taking them on the road and selling them out of the back of his station wagon. Success was his only option, and he didn't waver. Hal traveled across the country selling ladders to anyone who would buy.

The first four years on the road, my dad literally slept in his car. From time to time, Hal was asked to move from the spot where he had stopped to sleep, so he became used to short nights. He always carried an ice box with him on the road, and would often tell us that sometimes he went many days eating only cheese and crackers and some fruit.

This type of door-to-door selling worked well because Hal was passionate about his product, and once he demonstrated it, it was often a sure sale. Hal moved up to using a van to transport the ladders and kept on-the-road selling.

One night, Hal and Clark Butler had just left a trade show late at night with a van full of ladders when the police pulled them over. The police told Hal there had been a number of robberies in the area and asked what he had in the van. When Hal told him he had ladders, the police asked him to provide proof that the ladders were his. He explained that he built the ladders himself, so he had no documented proof that they were his. The police didn't believe him, so they told Hal they were taking him down to the station.

Hal's quick thinking and ingenuity kicked in, and he opened the back of the van. He whipped out a ladder and started showing the policemen how the ladder worked and all of the various features. He so impressed them that, not only were they fully convinced the ladders were his, but he even made a sale! One of the police officers bought a ladder right then and there. Now, that's taking success by storm.

For Hal, there was always an opportunity to be selling. He didn't wait for opportunities to present themselves. He took opportunities and turned them into sales.

During those early years my father spent, on average, more than 300 days out of the year on the road selling ladders. You'd think that those sales were the most important thing, but they actually weren't. What Hal was building was a foundation. He was building relationships that would serve him well into the future and act as a springboard for the success yet to come.

Halways:

- Success was Hal's only option, and he didn't waver.
- For Hal, there was always an opportunity to be selling.
- Hal didn't wait for opportunities to present themselves, he took opportunities and turned them into sales.
- Hal had a daily quota to meet, and he kept going until he made it...every single day.
- Hal never backed down from a challenge.
- Hal used his obstacles and setbacks as inspiration to look ahead and focus on what he could control instead of what he couldn't.

Hal How-Tos:

What can you do in your current position right now that could impact your success in that role?

Everyone is in sales. How can you use Hal's sales philosophy and approach to impact your success?

What are you willing to do to make the most of your situation and use it to climb up to the next rung of your career?

What relationships are you building that can serve you well both today and in the future?

"If you concentrate on building the business and not the man, you will not achieve. But, if you concentrate on building the man, you achieve both."

– Hal Wing

Little Giant Ladder employees outside the Provo, Utah facility (early 1980s)

CHAPTER TWO

The Secret to Becoming a Great Salesperson Is to Become a Great Person

Hal understood from an early age that people matter. His parents instilled in him the principles of hard work, organization, preparedness and charity. As much as Hal was building the Little Giant Ladder company with great products, he also was building the company with great character and, as a result, great people.

Hal sold a lot of ladders. Yes, they were a great product with a great design, but Hal had a secret weapon that made his ladders irresistible…himself. The relationships he built with his customers those first years set a firm foundation for the company's long-term success. Here's why.

He had The Hal Factor. Think of it as the "It Factor," Hal Wing-style. It not only made an impression, but it also influenced everyone he met. Klint Clausen, a longtime employee in the sales department, described Hal as someone you instantly fell in love with. "He was personable, and his energy was contagious," said Clausen. "You just wanted to be around him. He was honest and trustworthy; you knew it from the minute you met him."

Hal valued people. He genuinely wanted to help people and make their lives better. He knew his ladder was a vehicle to do that because of its commitment to quality and safety. What he knew was even more important was his word. His customers knew it, and that's why they bought from him. His employees knew it, and that is why many of them spent decades in his employ.

Mark Anderton, a former employee and fellow military member, said Hal's pillars of leadership came from the military. He commanded attention, yet he never raised his voice. He invested in people. He was a master communicator, but what made him stand out was his ability to listen. "When Hal was talking to you, you were the only one in the room," said Anderton. "He engaged with everyone. He was open and encouraged people to share their ideas. He never hesitated to let people come to what they needed to do on their own instead of dictating how he thought it should go."

Hal believed hard work was a virtue. He would often say that

"If you want to achieve a goal, you have to work five times harder."

He was always pushing, both in his business and in his personal life. Hal had an adventurous spirit. He liked to go fast, and he never let anything get in his way. He would often grab an employee and take them on a ride through the canyons.

His love of fast cars, motorcycles and dirt bikes was something he loved to share, and it was often said that no one ever got out of a car or off the back of a bike after riding with Hal without blue fingers from hanging on for dear life. That is how Hal approached life and business, with sheer gusto and a no-fear, no-fail attitude.

Hal dealt with things head-on and never wavered from his focus of making Little Giant Ladders the best in the world. His employees saw this every day and respected him for it, and they wanted to work harder because of it. His greatest asset, though, was not the product itself, but the people who were part of the company, and Hal truly lived that.

One time, Darius Penrod, a manufacturing employee with the company and the caretaker of Hal's many vehicles, had taken the trailer with a load of hay for Hal. The truck caught fire, and the truck, trailer and hay all burned right there on the side of the road. Darius was so scared to call Hal.

When he did, he started to quickly explain what happened, but Hal stopped him mid-sentence. He said calmly, "Darius, are you okay? The truck and trailer can be replaced. It's okay as long as you're okay." That character is the core of who Hal was as a person and as a leader.

Hal never let anyone forget that the success of the business was a team effort. He would say,

"All of you take me to the top of the mountain every day."

He really meant it. My dad would walk through the production facility every day and take time to speak with people. He knew everyone's name, and he knew them personally. He genuinely cared about their lives outside of work, and that made all the difference to everyone who worked there. They knew that Hal cared for them, and so they worked harder because of it. "Hal made all of us feel like we owned the company," said Mike O'Reilly, a longtime employee. Hal would tell his employees,

"This is your company, so if you want this thing to be successful, you better get your butt in gear and get going."

Little Giant was a family, and Hal treated everyone as such. Hal would take employees on vacation or pay for them to go on vacation all while paying them as if they were working. He gave everyone a chance. Because Hal faced his own challenges early on in life and was often bullied, he was a champion of the underdog. He hired people because he wanted to give them a chance.

On more than one occasion, Hal hired someone who maybe had trouble with the law, or things had gone badly somewhere else. That never deterred Hal, and some of his longest-term employees were those who Hal had taken a chance on, trusted and empowered to contribute. They, in turn, became some of the company's most valued assets.

Hal's sales genius was not limited to ladders. It extended to people. Everyone wanted to work at Little Giant. Why? Because of Hal Wing. Hal wanted people to do a good job instead of just working for a paycheck. He had high expectations and lived those expectations as an example, just as his parents had done. Hal wanted things a certain way, and he took the time to make sure everyone understood the importance of order, organization and integrity.

At Little Giant, much like growing up on the farm, everything had its place, and everything was neat and organized, even on the production floor. Everyone knew this and was expected to keep things tidy. One time, while Hal was out of town, the production manager let the place get messy. When Hal returned and went over to Little Giant to check on things, he got an eyeful. Though it was 1:00 in the morning, he promptly called the production manager to come over and clean things up right then and there. From then on, the production floor was always organized and clean.

Kevin Stephenson started in production and later moved into sales. He recalls that Hal would often say,

"A job worth doing is worth doing right."

People achieved more in his employ because they didn't want to disappoint Hal.

Jerry Jessen, a retired employee in the logistics department, said "Hal was ahead of his time in employee morale because of his principled leadership. What does that mean? It means he cared for and was engaged in employees' lives. He valued their contributions and recognized their role in his success."

Jerry continued, "I knew that Hal Wing loved me so much, and that made me want to work that much harder for him. I didn't want to disappoint him or let him down."

When Mike O'Reilly was hired, he had a really run-down vehicle. Hal said to Mike, "If you're going to work here, you need a good vehicle. Go to the dealership and pick out a truck. If you work for me for five years, the truck is yours." Mike bought the truck he wanted, and five years later, the truck was given to Mike free and clear.

In all of his success, Hal never forgot the sacrifices he made early on in the life of Little Giant. Being on the road 300 days per year, sleeping in his station wagon and eating packed meals from home and cheese and crackers to get by, he knew what he gained, and he knew what he missed. Mel Huffaker, a 25-year employee in the sales department recalls how Hal valued the sales department. He said,

"The sales department is the engine of the company. There is no reason to build one ladder until someone sells one."

That didn't mean repeating history. Hal knew that Mel had a young family. Because Mel was on the road selling and attending trade shows, he was away from home quite a bit. Hal went to him and said, "I know how precious time is with family. When the sales team is on the road, you're working. When you're not on the road, you're to be at home with your family."

"That made all the difference to the salespeople, and it made everyone work harder for him," said Mel.

Family was important to Hal. Everything he did was for his family. He extended that same mindset to his employees and his community. I can remember one time an employee was fired by a department head, and it was Christmas time. My dad called me into his office, and he said, "Doug, I want you to take this check to the employees house. Even though we had to fire him, it's Christmas and without a paycheck, there will probably be no gifts for his family. I want them to have a good Christmas, so deliver this check to him."

So, I drove to the man's house. When I knocked on the door, his young daughter answered. I asked for her dad, and he came to the door looking pretty angry. I simply handed him the check and told him my dad wanted him and his family to have a Merry Christmas. I can only imagine the look on his face when he opened that envelope and found a check.

There are so many stories like this I can tell. In all of the interviews I have conducted, I have learned more about my dad than I ever even knew, not just about the business man that he was, but the person he was. Mike O'Reilly tells a story of delivering a $20,000 check to a woman with five children whose husband had just passed away. Hal found out how much was owed on her mortgage and gave her the money to pay it off. "To this day, when I see that woman, she thinks it was me who gave her that money," says O'Reilly, "and I still tell her it wasn't me. That's who Hal was. He didn't want any recognition. He only wanted to help people."

Terry Penrod, a longtime employee, shared with me how my dad heard on the radio that a farmer who lived a town over from us had lost all of his hay. Without hesitation, my dad loaded up a semi-trailer full of hay and had it delivered to the farmer. Anonymously, of course.

People have come up to me and told me that my dad put a new roof on their home, that he bought them a car, or took care of some big expense. One widow even told me that my dad bought her a house. Such incredible gestures of kindness and love, and no one ever knew about them. He never sought praise, only to share the blessings of what he had with others. As Mark Anderton recalled, "Hal had made it, but he would never tell you that he made it."

As Hal said,

"You will become what you invest in your life."

Halways:

- Hal valued people. He genuinely wanted to help people and make their lives better.
- Hal was personable, honest and trustworthy. People just wanted to be around him.
- Hal believed hard work was a virtue.
- Hal had a no-fear, no-fail attitude
- Hal never let anyone forget that the success of the business was a team effort.
- Hal would often say, "A job worth doing is worth doing right."

Hal How-Tos:

How does who you are as a person affect your performance at work? Are you respected? Are you a leader? If not, how can you change that?

What traits do you have as a person that can make you better at what you do? How can you use some of these same principles to advance your career or grow your business?

What is your energy like at work, with colleagues and customers? Do you attract people to you with your personality and focus?

Are you offering to do more than is required of you? Do you go out of your way to help others in your company succeed? How do you think taking those types of actions could help you in your position or career?

Do you go out of your way to help a customer get information or find a product they need? Are you connecting with them and making additional recommendations about other products that would help them while increasing your sales?

"Sometimes we all need a check up from the neck up."

– Hal Wing

This chapel now sits on land that was once a part of my dad's farm (2016)

CHAPTER THREE
Choose to Love What You Do

Hal was extremely perceptive. He really had a gift of being able to read people. Somehow, he instinctively knew what people needed and how they were feeling. He identified with all different types of people, and preferred the company of his employees and family to business tycoons and millionaires.

That grounded and rooted footing Hal had was from his foundation in his faith and in his church. Hal lived by example. It was never so much that he told people about his faith as much as he lived a faithful life.

My dad always told me that we were blessed, not because of anything special we did, but we were blessed with financial means. With that came a big responsibility to bless the lives of other people. He believed our blessings weren't ours but something we were blessed with in order to bless others. This wasn't only limited to finances but also included our time, gifts and service to our community and our church. Hal would often volunteer himself and all of us kids to go help out on the church's sugar beet farms. The harvest from those farms helped serve families all across the area.

Later on in life, part of Hal and Brigitte's service to the church was missionary work in Germany. As the Harper's, mission president and leaders of the Germany Munich Mission for the Church of Jesus Christ of Latter Day Saints remembered, Hal and Brigitte were assigned to a loveless, challenging congregation in Kaufbeuren. They dove right in, though, thinking outside the box and leading by example to bring more people and new energy to the congregation. Their "Linger

Longer" program in particular drew new people and had people at the church sharing and in fellowship long after the Sunday service concluded. The changes my parents created at that church altered its trajectory and the dynamic of those who attended there. It was so successful, in fact, that upon returning to Utah, the church asked Hal and Brigitte to train missionaries taking assignments in Germany and Europe, which they did for about two years.

Back in Utah, Hal always had his pulse on the community. No matter how busy he was, he made time to care for those in need. He knew that one day, he would have to make an account for how he used the gifts God gave him, and he was determined to help make people's lives better and to give them chances and opportunities they might not otherwise have.

Jina Tibbets experienced this first hand. While donating blood at a local blood drive, she passed out. Hal was there checking people in and sprang into action. Jina's little girl was with her, and she was scared, so Hal comforted her and talked to her, reassuring her that her mom was going to be okay. Once Jina was feeling better, Hal personally took her and her daughter home. "It was always the feeling that Hal left people with. They knew that he really cared for them. It was humbling," said Jina.

At home, he and Brigitte led the family in daily scripture reading and prayer. Brigitte would even pray in German. Hal believed that this set the same example for his children that his parents set for him. He would always tell us kids,

"We're doing pretty well on our own, but with God's help, we can do so much better."

I believe this scripture embodies Hal Wing.

"Seek ye first the kingdom of God and his righteousness and all these things shall be added unto you." Matthew 6:33

Today, when I drive by the two chapels our church built in Springville, I am reminded of my dad and this verse. He donated the land on which these chapels sit. They are right across the street from each other on what was once my father's farm—the same farm Hal once mortgaged to invest in Little Giant. So for me, it is a monumental reminder of what my dad believed and how he lived his life.

At Little Giant, too, Hal lived by example. Every meeting started with a word of prayer. At Christmas, every year, we held a traditional Christmas party. Hal would address all of the employees and have someone read from the Bible. Being sensitive to everyone's feelings, he would tell the employees what they were about to do, so if anyone was uncomfortable with it, they could step out. But, he never apologized for it or held back in his faith.

For a few years, Hal was mayor of our town, Springville, Utah. He was known for starting every meeting with prayer. Upon hearing of this, the ACLU sent Hal a letter and told him he was not to pray while in service to the city or else they would sue him. I can remember my dad saying, literally, "Bring it on. I am not going to stop praying before meetings." So pray they did. No suit was ever brought. This is just another example of the "forge ahead with strong convictions, no fear, only faith" grasp my dad had on life.

It was this unshakable faith that ultimately carried over into Hal's belief in himself. People look at Little Giant now and see all of the success, but that wasn't always the case. There were some really hard times. There were times when it wasn't clear we would make it, but my dad never showed fear. He had faith and confidence that we would for sure be successful, and he never once wavered on that faith and belief. I do think that played a role. Hal's unbelievable work ethic, his faith and confidence in himself and the company's potential gave everyone at Little Giant that same confidence and kept us on a consistent path that led us to where we are today.

Halways:

- Hal had a gift of being able to read people and was extremely perceptive.
- Hal gave his time, gifts and service to his church and his community.
- Hal had unshakable faith in God, himself and his company. He never showed fear or wavered in that faith.
- Hal had a strong work ethic and always stayed focused on his goals.

Hal How Tos:

What are your guiding principles?

How do your principles impact your career and professional relationships?

Do you go to work with a great attitude and a sincere commitment to doing your best? If not, how do you think shifting your mindset and actions could impact your success?

What do you do to help colleagues and customers every day?

Do you have an unshakable faith in your ability to be successful? If not, try this: Make a list of your best characteristics, habits and past accomplishments. Begin to apply each of these to your current position and see how they can help you in your day-to-day tasks.

"Don't lie, don't steal and don't be lazy."

– Hal Wing

My dad and I at Bonneville Raceways in
Salt Lake City, Utah (1983)

CHAPTER FOUR

Your Moral Compass Determines Your Direction

Hal had a reputation that preceded him. Mike O'Reilly, a longtime employee, said, "Hal was a man's man. He was one of those guys you either liked or you didn't. I liked him because he was upfront and honest. I thought this guy is as honest as any person I've ever known."

Hal was certainly direct. If you asked him a question, he wasn't going to tell you what you wanted to hear; he was going to tell you the truth. That carried over into the business. Hal would walk through the office and the production facility on a regular basis talking to employees, asking them how things were going and what adjustments needed to be made. "When Hal asked you a question, he really wanted to know the answer," recalls O'Reilly. "He actually listened and never interrupted you. Whoever he was speaking to had his complete focus and attention."

Hal was the first one to pat you on the back and offer praise, and also the first one to chew you out if you needed it—and that applied to *everyone*. I can remember one time my dad and mom went out to dinner, and my brothers and I were at the shop working. At Little Giant, everyone punches in when they get to work and punches out when they leave. We were no different. We arrived at Little Giant, punched in, and I got to work cleaning the bathrooms (since that was my job). My brothers decided they were going to pull their car in and wash it. I knew this wasn't a good idea, so I stuck to bathroom duty.

My dad had a way of knowing things. I will never understand it. Whether it was promptings, premonitions or what, he just knew things. Sometimes, that was a great thing. Today was not one of those days. While at dinner, Hal had a sense that he needed to come check on us, so on the way home from dinner, they stopped by Little Giant. I was in the bathroom scrubbing away, and all of a sudden I heard yelling. It was my dad's voice, so I didn't dare venture out.

A few minutes later, my dad stormed into the bathroom to check on me. He said to me, "Oh good, you're working. Good thing because I just fired your brothers." He asked me how long I was going to be, and he and my mom worked in the office until I was done so I could ride home with them.

My father treated us kids just like everyone else, and when we screwed up, we paid the price. Thankfully, I had older siblings who sometimes got in trouble and taught me what not to do, so I only got in trouble a few times. When it did happen though, my dad would always come back and talk to each of us about what we did wrong and why it was wrong. Most importantly, he always told us that, no matter what, he loved us. That is what stuck with me the most.

"I didn't build this company to be rich, I built it so I could work with my sons."

This is something Hal said from the very beginning. He was building not just a company, but a legacy. He took family and work very seriously, and although it was difficult for him to have to discipline us or fire us, he knew it was necessary to learn lessons of honesty, trustworthiness and work ethic.

Throughout his entire life, my dad loved working with his children at Little Giant. My older brother and I chose to spend our entire careers at the company. Dad recognized each of our unique gifts early on and helped us grow so we could help him expand the company. I know he had a deep sense of pride having his children by his side at Little Giant. Even today, the company continues to be guided by the Wing family and leadership handpicked and mentored by Hal.

Along the way, Hal had several offers to buy Little Giant. The Werner Ladder Company (the largest ladder company in the world) offered to buy the company at least four times, but my dad always said no. He remembered what the Werners had said to him when he was just starting out, and he always said he would never sell to them.

I can remember once, though, a great offer came in from a private equity group based in New York, so my dad agreed to meet with them. Here come six suits in a private jet flying in from New York to meet with my dad. They arrived at the office and settled in the conference room. My dad came in and sat down. After about 15 minutes of exchange, my dad looked at the principal of the company and said, "What happens to all of my employees when I sell?"

The gentleman casually answered that they would have a job for a while until outsourcing could be put in place. At that point, all manufacturing would be sent overseas and our people let go. Hal stood up and said,

> **"I am responsible for the families of every one of the people here. I promised them they would always have their jobs, and I am not going back on that promise. I am sorry you came all this way because I am not selling."**

Stunned, the principal of the company said to Hal, "Don't you know how much money we are offering you?" Hal calmly replied, "I already have enough money. I love these people too much to do this to them. Good-day, gentlemen."

The suits tried to reason with my dad, but he was done with the conversation and left the room. He walked away from a lot of money that day, but he made a commitment to his people, and he was not going to go back on it for anything.

Hal was known for always knowing what he wanted the end game to be. Robin Hartl Trout worked with Hal on our infomercial and said, "Hal followed specific steps to get where he wanted to go. If anything got in his way, he just rerouted and kept going."

My dad believed that there was nothing in life that should stop you from pursuing what you want. He always said there would be challenges and difficulties, but that we should always keep plugging away with the end goal in mind. Almost everyone I spoke with when writing this biography got that same message from my dad and relayed it back to me either in a story or in an interaction with Hal. He was definitely consistent.

My dad believed that you lived by your word. In the early days of Little Giant, it was my dad out on the road, selling ladders and cultivating relationships. Our ladders were built using only high-quality materials by people who lived in our community in Utah. If my dad said our ladder could do something, it did it. If my dad told a customer their order would be delivered by a certain date, that deadline was met.

Yes, that sometimes meant my dad was out on the floor assembling ladders right along with the production team (and me, by this point). If my dad acquired a new customer, they were treated like family right away. That was why, even though you could buy a competitor's ladder for much less, my dad was able to literally create a whole new ladder category, selling them for more than three times the price of other ladders. It was this commitment to integrity and honesty that helped catapult Little Giant Ladders to great success.

I've already told you my dad had a great sense about things. Hal loved spending time out on the road visiting customers all throughout his career. He also was very engaged in every step of the manufacturing process to ensure we were delivering a quality product on every order.

One evening, Hal got the sense things weren't quite right at Little Giant. He went out on the production floor to inspect the ladders, only to find that they were not being assembled to the standard he expected. Right then and there, he stopped production and scrapped 800 ladders—literally completely pulling them from production and starting over! This meant all new material and time to rebuild them, but Hal stood fast. We would only deliver the best ladders in the world, no matter the cost. There was absolutely no room for shortcuts. Needless to say, that never happened again, and the order was fulfilled and delivered to the customers on time.

Even with Hal's strong work ethic, he made time to play. His love of cars and dirt bikes often made rides mobile meetings. Scott Finlayson, former police chief of Springville, went dirt biking with Hal on several occasions. "I was terrible at dirt biking, but I went because I knew that in the hour drive there and the hour drive back, I would have Hal's complete attention. We accomplished a lot and had some great conversations. Once we were on those bikes, though, it was crazy. I could not keep up with him. The faster Hal went, the happier he was."

The first time Scott met Hal he went to his office to ask for a donation of a car to use for the police department's D.A.R.E. program. After meeting with Hal for just a few minutes, Hal picked up the phone, called a friend who owned a dealership and had a car waiting for Scott to pick up. "That is a perfect example of how Hal did things and how he supported his community. We wrapped and used that car for many years."

Scott also recalled advising Hal on his run for mayor. "I told him that I didn't think he would like being mayor because of the city's process on things. Hal was a doer. If he decided something needed to be done, he did it right now. The city did not work like that. Almost nothing was ever done quickly."

As mayor, Hal brought the same work ethic and integrity to the city office as he did at Little Giant. Scott recalls Hal "cleaning house" at the city because people were not willing to change to do things honestly and with transparency. "Hal was not willing to compromise his ethics in any area, including city hall." Needless to say, Scott was correct. My dad quickly became frustrated with the slow pace of government and resigned his post during his first term.

"Even though Hal did not serve a full term," Scott recalled, "He was able to put the city's finances back on track. Even today, the city would be struggling financially without the people and processes Hal put into place back then."

Halways:

- Hal was upfront and honest.
- When Hal spoke with someone, they had his full attention and never interrupted.
- Hal always knew what he wanted the end game to be.
- Hal believed that you lived by your word.
- Hal was a doer. When he decided something needed to be done, he got it done right away.

Hal How-Tos:

Think about your own communication style. Do you listen intently when people speak? Are you focused on what they are saying or what you are going to say next? This is so important when dealing with both customers and employees.

What are your goals? What do you want your end game to be? Write it down. What can you do today to further those goals down the field?

What do you want to be known for? When you say you'll do something, is it done? Are you reliable, credible and trustworthy? These attributes greatly affect your ability to sell successfully.

Do you wait for someone to tell you to do something, or do you take initiative when you see something needs attention? Try it today, and see what happens.

Do you look for ways to be more valuable to your employer or team? If not, what can you do to begin that process?

"You can tell the customer anything you want to, as long as it's the truth."

– Hal Wing

The first Little Giant sales team. Left to right; Dan Miller, Gary Donaldson, Ron Jensen, Hal Wing, Clark Butler, Dan Morgan, Clyde Morgan (1979)

CHAPTER FIVE

When You Tell the Truth, You'll Never Have to Remember What You Said

In all of the interviews I did for this book, there were a few resounding responses about my dad. The first was how he loved people and how much he cared for everyone around him. The second was Hal's integrity.

In 1981, Hal received an opportunity to sell the company to another business in California and he took their offer. This organization owned multiple companies and said they were only interested in keeping the business based right here in Utah.

By 1986, things started to go downhill. It became known that Little Giant had become victim to a Ponzi scheme, and the owners were just sucking the cash out of all the businesses they held. Little Giant collapsed.

Hal took action right away. He went into the Central Bank in town to talk with the bank president, Mr. Calvin Packard. Matt Packard, now president of the bank and an advisor to the board of Little Giant, recalls the story. "Whenever Hal walked into the bank, everybody knew him, and he spoke to everyone. He had a larger-than-life personality. This particular day, he had an appointment with my father who was then president of the bank. Hal explained what happened to Little Giant. He told my father that he had no assets but that he needed one million dollars from the bank to buy back Little Giant and get the business going again. He promised that he would pay the bank back every cent. Because of Hal's integrity and his honesty, my father gave him that one million dollars right then and there on a handshake. Hal paid back every cent he borrowed that day, just as my father knew he would."

Hal knew the value of relationships. He knew the value of honesty and integrity, and most importantly, he knew he could not revive Little Giant without his vendors and suppliers. Once Hal had the business back, the next step was getting the suppliers back on line.

The problem was vendors had provided materials and services but were never paid. Hal went and visited every vendor personally and explained the situation. He then promised each one that he would pay them everything they were owed by the previous owners if they would continue supplying materials to Little Giant. All but one of them agreed.

They did so because they knew my dad, they trusted him, they knew he had great integrity and his word was credible. My dad was able to get the business fully functional quickly, almost like it had never faltered. I asked my dad once, "Wasn't it harder the second time?"

He replied,

"No, it was easier. I identified all of my past mistakes and eliminated them."

Did my dad have to pay the bills of the previous owner? No, he didn't. It wasn't he who ran the company into the ground. Yet, he took full responsibility for the brand the minute he got the company back, and he was determined to not only succeed but build the company bigger, stronger and even better than before. And he did just that.

It wasn't just the vendors Hal took care of. There also were hundreds of customers who had outstanding orders for Little Giant Ladders under the previous ownership. When the company went bankrupt, all of those orders went unfulfilled. That is, until Hal took over. Once he purchased the assets back and the new business was established, Hal had the customer service team reach out to every customer with an outstanding order and assured them that their orders would be fulfilled. Again, my dad did not not have to do that, but he knew it was the right thing to do. It was how he and Little Giant operated, and it was the foundation upon which their success was built.

My father's word was everything, and he never went back on it. This is just one of the reasons he became so successful. Had he not been an honest and ethical man every day, he never would have gotten the money to buy back Little Giant, and the company would not even exist today. Sometimes, it's the things you consistently do and say along the way when nobody's watching, that will influence the direction of your life, the opportunities that present themselves and your road to success. As Matt recalled my dad saying,

> **"Look at the issues from the perspective of 100 years. What will be the right answer in not one year, or ten years, but 100 years. That's the right answer."**

Hal's credibility and ethics modeled the behavior of everyone at Little Giant. He would often say,

> **"I only work half a day. Twelve hours is good enough for anybody."**

The fact is, my father rarely slept. I can recall on several occasions he would call me at two o' clock in the morning and ask me what I was doing. He had an idea and wanted to talk.

When I told him it was two in the morning, and that I was asleep he would say, "Oh, I'm sorry, I forget that you sleep." Hal would regularly only sleep two to three hours per night, but he was always energized and hustling at the office.

He was always available, walking the floor, talking with employees, helping the sales team, interacting with customers and checking the quality of the product. It was important for him that every ladder that left our facility lived up to its promise and exceeded expectations. They did have his name on them, and he never took that lightly.

As his children working in the business, neither did we. It wasn't because we had anything to prove to anyone but because we always wanted to make our dad proud and live up to his values, ethics and integrity. That work ethic and life philosophy guides each of us to this day.

A salesman himself, Hal was a champion for the guys in the sales department. He often referred to them as the engine of the company. Hal would go to shows and do demonstrations better than anyone. Dan Miller, a former salesman with the company, at one time held the record for 167 ladders sold at one show. Hal taught him exactly what to do.

"The secret," explained Dan, "was the demonstration. There is no better way to sell the ladder because it sold itself. The proof is in the pudding when you're showing people what the ladder can do, how it is constructed and how much it can hold. We'd get several people climbing up on the ladders right there on the show floor to demonstrate just how high quality our ladders were and how reliable. The sales process always started with a detailed scripted demonstration. You could never tell the price of the ladder before the demonstration," said Miller.

Remember, at this time, you could go to the store and buy a ladder for $30 or $40. The Little Giant Ladders were around

$300. When people would ask how much the ladder cost, my dad would go into show mode, demonstrating all of the features and benefits of the ladder.

In fact, Hal even scripted out the entire demonstration for the sales team. But there was no one who could show it like Hal. His energy and enthusiasm was unmatched. In fact, while on the sales floor, he never took a break. We had to remind him that the guys working the booth had to take time out for bathroom breaks and lunch. "Eating is a waste of time," Hal would say.

Craig Willet, a former board member at Little Giant, recalls Hal's philosophy on selling to customers:

1. Make sure you have a great product
2. Make sure the customer understands your product and how it works.
3. Be able to demonstrate the features and benefits of the product.
4. Understand the needs of the customer, and make sure that customer understands how your product can benefit them, reinforcing the value of it.
5. Don't make a product with subtle differences. Deliver a product that is totally unique.
6. Don't give your product away. Hal would always say,

"We know our value. Never badmouth the competition, just show them why we're better."

It worked every time.

Halways:

- If you are honest and ethical every day, that reputation will serve you well in times of need.
- Keep your word, and always do the right thing.
- Play the long game. What is the right answer 100 years from now?
- Don't tell people how great your product is, show them.
- Never badmouth the competition.

Hal How-Tos:

Do a self-assessment. Do you do what you say you're going to do? Do you live up to your word? Are you ethical and honest when no one is looking?

How do you model your behavior? Does it set a good example for others? Do you take on a leadership role all on your own?

What is your work style? Are you hustling every day? Are you open to new assignments and opportunities in your current role? Do you proactively try to help others and the company with ideas, support and feedback?

Do you know your product inside and out? Do you understand how it compares to competitive products? Do you take the time to match a product with a customer's needs?

"Never forget: the products make us all look good."

– Hal Wing

Hal Wing at a trade show on the top of a Little Giant
Skyscraper ladder. (1979)

CHAPTER SIX

Passion Transfers All the Way to the Cash Register

When Hal Wing brought the Little Giant Ladder to the market, it created a whole new category of ladder that did not exist before. For the first few years, Hal was out on the road, selling ladders face-to-face. As the company grew, Hal never took his eye off the sales ball. In fact, he loved the work so much, he kept on doing right to the end.

Sometimes, Hal would hear grumblings from production about how much money the sales guys made each year. Not one to shy away from anything, Hal addressed it at a company meeting. He said, "These guys have to know the product inside and out, travel with it, demonstrate it over and over, work show booths for 12-plus hours a day and be on the road away from their families for weeks at a time. If any of you are willing to give up that time with your family and take on that workload, come see me about getting into sales." Almost no one did.

While Hal was partial to the department he was passionate about, he was also a stickler for detail. Every year, Hal held a sales "Hal (hell) Week." The sales team had to come in off the road and spend a week building ladders in the production facility. Hal always rolled up his sleeves and built right along with them—and me and my brother and the rest of the production team. It not only set a good example for the rest of the staff, it gave everyone an appreciation for the others' jobs. Kevin Stephenson, a salesman for the company for 25 years shared, "Even into his sixties, Hal was building ladders right along with his people."

In fact, my dad had worked so much in manufacturing over the years, his hearing was permanently damaged because he never thought to wear ear protection. When that week was over, though, there was not a question any prospect or customer could ask that a Little Giant salesman could not answer. Then, it was back on the road.

My dad loved working with customers, and he loved demonstrating our ladders. Now for context, it is important to know that my dad was not a big man. He was about five foot seven and about 160 pounds, but he twirled that ladder like it was a baton.

It wasn't until later, after Hal was gone, that we developed lightweight ladders. Little Giant was always investing in innovation. When we were challenged by the NCTA committee, consisting of all of the cable and telecom companies, to build an extension ladder that reduced weight from 100 to 50 pounds, we approached the project with the same confidence, grit and no-fail attitude Hal embodied. Using his principles and commitment to quality, our innovation in building a lighter yet strong ladder led to a huge breakthrough in the industry.

Little Giant Ladders are strong but light, weighing in at about 48 pounds while competitor products weigh in at more than 100 pounds. This has become a huge selling point. Not only do companies save millions in the reduction of injuries and workmen's compensation claims, but our ladder opened up a whole new world of opportunities in the trades for women.

Let's look closer at what we did for the cable television industry. Anyone who has cable has had to have the company come out and install or do repairs. What do they always have strapped to the top of the van? A ladder. Because every call requires removing, moving and replacing that ladder on the top of the van, it was almost impossible for women to serve as technicians. It was almost always men; until Little Giant Ladders came along. The lighter weight, easy to manage ladders gave women the ability to secure technician jobs and take care of their families. Hal always said,

> **"The most important thing I can offer anyone is opportunity."**

Over the course of time, other products have come out that tried to copy Little Giant. My dad was never afraid of competition. He would say,

> **"When competitors copy us, it is the greatest form of flattery. When they stop copying us, that is the time we should be worried."**

That suited everyone fine until Mr. Kim from Korea came along with the WK ladder made in China that looked and functioned just like a Little Giant. The worst part was that it retailed for $99, less than half of what one of our ladders cost at retail. Everyone was nervous. The overseas company hired away one of our best sales guys and attended all the same trade shows we did. Over the course of the next several months, our sales started to drop. Everyone started getting scared and worried, including me. The only one who never showed any fear was my dad. I would ask him what he thought about it, and he told me this:

> **"We've always made it, and we're always going to make it."**

I have to admit, I was still nervous. Instead of feeling defeated or getting anxious, my dad did the opposite. He addressed it with the entire company. Hal went out and bought one of the WK ladders and brought it to a full company meeting. He looked it over carefully, and upon close inspection, he started to twist each side of the ladder in opposite directions. With seemingly not much force, the rungs popped and the welds broke and flew off of the ladder. My dad stood back with a look of satisfaction on his face. The whole staff was quiet and amazed. One, because, as I mentioned, my dad was not a big guy and second, because at that moment, we all realized this ladder was total junk. My dad explained that in China, they do not understand nor know how to weld like we do here in America, so when even a moderate amount of pressure was placed on the rungs, they popped. The WK ladders got out into the field, they broke, people got injured and the company was out of business within a year's time.

Once again, Hal did not badmouth the competition nor did he panic. He just did what he always did. He stayed focused on his product, its quality and his integrity.

In another product knock-off story, the Werner Ladder Company came out with a ladder that had a similar look and functionality. Little Giant's biggest industrial customer, Grainger Industrial Supply, called and said they wanted to see Klint and me (we were their contacts) in three weeks. They had the Werner Ladder there, and they wanted us to come in and demonstrate why their customers should pay more than double for our ladder over the Werner. If we could not convince them that ours was worth the price, they were going to go exclusively with Werner.

Klint Clausen, the Little Giant sales rep that handled the Grainger account, called me and was very nervous. What could we say or show them that would convince them? How would the meeting go? I followed my dad's lead. First, I prayed about what we should do in this meeting.

On meeting day, we took in a Werner ladder that we had cut into pieces. We showed them the difference in the materials of the two ladders, including the thickness of the material and the mechanisms that adjust the ladders. Then, we focused on the welds. We showed them our welds and compared them to the Werner ladder, which, because it was made in China, was riveted. Like the earlier WK ladder, those rivets could not withstand wear and tear and easily tore out of the material when twisted. We also told them that, after 30 years in business, we never had a recall on our ladders. We explained to them that we did not want to lose their business, but it was up to them. Grainger kept us on.

My dad had a long history with the Werner family. Remember, they originally told Hal he was a fool and would not succeed. Then, they tried to buy the company multiple times. It all came full circle when, at a show, one of the Werner brothers said to me, "Doug, if you ever tell anyone this, I'll deny it, but I have one of your ladders at my house. It's the Little Giant Safety Step ladder." He also went on to tell me how much he respected my dad. That meant a great deal to me.

There is room in the market for everyone. So, if you own a business or are selling a product, don't badmouth a competitor. Instead, focus on the attributes of your product that will make people see the value and motivate them to purchase. Then, you'll be smiling all the way to the bank.

Halways

- Stay strong in your belief and never let your team see you waver in that belief.
- Focus on what makes your product better and showcase it.
- Don't fear competition. Hal believed that imitation is the greatest form of flattery.
- When your employees/colleagues are scared or there is tension, deal with it head-on using facts and truths, not emotion.

Hal How-Tos:

In your current role, are you the kind of leader you want others to be; a boss, for example?

When faced with a challenge, how do you handle it? Do you get upset? Do you give up? Are you defeated? How does how you approach and deal with difficult situations affect those around you? How does it impact your position?

When customers question you or have a problem, do you deal with it right away head-on, or do you avoid their calls? How can you equip yourself to address tough issues and keep customers loyal?

"The most important assets we have are not the patents, not the products or the buildings. Our people are our most important asset that we have at Little Giant."

– Hal Wing

Hal Wing with manufacturing employee Angela Baca (2005)

CHAPTER SEVEN
People, the Most Important Asset

Hal really lived and breathed this quote. I think maybe it was because he was bullied as a teen and felt isolated. He made it a point as an adult to make sure people were given chances, and they knew they deserved to be treated well, given respect and judged not for what they looked like but what they were willing to work for and what they accomplished.

In interviews, Hal always asked this question,

"Do you want a job, or do you want to work?

Hal never hired anyone who said they wanted a job. After all, his name was on the door, and he wanted people who wanted to accomplish something great with him. That's really how he looked at it; that the whole team was on this wild ride together.

When my father started hiring people at Little Giant, he always rooted for the underdog. If you lived on a farm, you were hired almost immediately. Being a farm boy himself, Hal knew those kids knew their way around hard work. If you were a wrestler, cross country runner or an Eagle Scout, Hal knew you had a strong work ethic so you pretty much had a job. He also never hesitated to hire people with a troubled past. On more than one occasion, Hal hired someone who had served time in prison.

In the early days of Little Giant, Hal and the human resources manager were going over resumes in preparation to hire new employees. The HR manager removed a resume, crinkled it into a ball, threw it into the wastebasket, and exclaimed, "We don't need to bring this person in for an interview, he's a loser." My dad walked over to the wastebasket and said, "What do you mean this guy is a loser?" The HR director told my dad that this person had just been released from prison. My dad quickly scanned the resume and noticed that the candidate was an Eagle Scout, and that he had served an honorable two-year church mission for his church.

My dad told the manager, "Let's bring him in for an interview." The candidate was not only hired, but he was an excellent employee, eventually became a manager, worked for Little Giant for more than 15 years and retired with the company. While most people probably would not have even gotten an interview, Hal made a point to meet with these unlikely candidates and feel them out to recognize their true potential. These often were some of the best hires the company made with multiple employees staying with the company the rest of their career. It says a lot about second chances, doesn't it? My father did not believe in judgment. He believed in opportunity.

Speaking of second chances, one of our best distributors in the San Francisco area, Phil James, very successfully sold Little Giant ladders for us. When a multi-purpose folding ladder from China came out, Phil called up my dad and told him he would no longer be carrying Little Giant, as he was going to go with the lower-priced copy ladder. My dad told him that was fine, but before he hung up he said to him, "Phil, I'm going to squash you like a bug."

Well, as you read earlier, those knock-off ladders were junk and didn't last long. Eight months later, my dad got a call from Phil. He said, "Hal, you told me you'd squash me like a bug, and that's exactly what you did. Now, can I have my job back?"

Hal calmly said, "Welcome back, Phil," and hung up the phone.

Craig Willet gave me this great insight into my dad's ability to connect with people and value each individually. He said, "Hal had to experience some lonely times, some times of rejection and inadequacy to where he could reach inside of himself and find who he was. Somebody who can do that the way Hal did can help other people find themselves."

Steve and Vicky Curtis know well the ability for Hal to see the value in people. When Steve was hurt on the job at his place of employment and lost his leg, Hal was right there almost immediately at the hospital offering love and support. Vicky explains, "I don't even know how Hal knew Steve was in the hospital, but he just showed up in his hospital room and started washing the dirt from the accident off of Steve's face and arms. I asked him how he got back here, and Hal casually said, "I just told them I was his brother, because in God's eyes, I am his brother."

Once Steve was on the mend, Hal called him up and offered him a job. When Steve pushed back because he could not be useful in the production facility, Hal said sternly, "Well, you can talk on the phone, can't you? Be here tomorrow. You have a job in customer service." The two men became lifelong friends and traveled together on many trips.

"Hal was always two steps ahead of everyone," said Steve. "While most people were talking about [steps] B & C, Hal was all the way at [step] H. That said, he never expected anyone to do anything he wasn't willing to do himself."

That rang true in every area of the business and in his personal life. Hal always said that

"With great reward, comes great responsibility. What we have is only on loan to us to help bless

others, and one day, we will have to give an account for how we used what we had been given in this life."

While Hal was big on opportunity and second chances, he had high expectations of his employees, and he didn't shy away from disciplinary action when needed. When I sat down with Dan Miller, a former salesman, he had quite the story to tell.

"I was a good salesman. In fact, I sold 167 ladders at one show. When I was scheduled to go to a trade show in Oklahoma one year, I didn't go because my wife was pregnant. My brother called and asked me to come out to his ranch for the afternoon, so I went. While I was there, I got a call from Hal asking me why I wasn't at the trade show. I told him why, and he told me I was fired. I honestly couldn't believe it. I was shocked. It really turned out to be a blessing, though, because I ended up starting my own shop which I would've never done had I kept that job. Hal and I eventually remained friends. In fact, he continued to send me commission checks for every ladder I ever sold, even after he fired me."

According to Dave Francis, who still works at Little Giant today, Hal put such a huge emphasis on people because he understood that if one succeeded, we all succeeded. "Hal's German attention to detail and quality drove him. He never wanted his ladders to just pass or be close to the line. He wanted Little Giant to be a legacy product, and he knew he could not accomplish that without a great team of people with him."

While Dave was on the road for three weeks, Hal showed up to Dave's new home and talked to his wife Lorie. They had just purchased the house, and they did not have the money for landscaping. Hal told Lorie to go and pick out what they wanted for their landscaping, and said he was going to pay for everything. "My wife and I were overwhelmed with gratitude," Dave shared. "To have that type of appreciation and kindness is so rare."

Dave once hired a man in his 50's to work on a machine in the plant. Dave told the man that the owner of the company may stop and talk with him while he was at work that day. At the end of the shift, the man came to Dave, and he had been crying. "Hal had stopped and spent several minutes with this man, just getting to know him and asking about his family," Dave said. "The man told me that he was moved to tears because no one had ever shown him that they cared about him that much."

On another occasion, Hal was walking through the production facility and noticed one of the worker's watches. This particular gentleman had worked for the company for 25 years and always commented on how much he liked Hal's watches. On this day, he approached the man who kindly told Hal how much he liked his watch. Hal looked at both watches and said,

"Really, I was just thinking how much I like your watch. Let's trade."

Hal literally traded a Rolex for a Timex that day and left smiling.

Hal's judge of character went beyond where someone was from or what he thought their potential could be. A perfect example is Brandon Moss. After working for Little Giant for a few years, Brandon had decided to take a job and move to Washington. Hal sat him down and told him that he thought the move was a mistake and that Brandon had great potential and a future at Little Giant. "Hal convinced me to stay, and that literally changed my life," said Brandon. "I would've never met my wife or had my kids. The fact is, Hal thought more about me than even I thought about myself, my potential and what I could accomplish. I try to think of that now in other situations. We shouldn't be too quick to judge because the person someone is now may not reflect the person they could be or what they could do."

Brandon went on to run the customer service department, growing it from two or three people to 28 people. He then assisted Hal with special projects and today, he works in the marketing department. His evolution has been extraordinary, and it's all thanks to Hal Wing.

Hal extended his expectations to his business partners and vendors. He often decided who he would do business with based on cleanliness. On several occasions, Hal would send people out to scout shops and plants to see their operation before we did any business with them. If their production facility, office or shop was dirty or unorganized, it was a no-go for Hal. He wanted to do business with people who shared his vision and values.

According to Hal, there are two types of employees you have to watch for:

1. The employee who doesn't want to do what they're told, and
2. The employee who only does what they're told.

My dad always went to bat for his employees and respect was a requirement in our office. When a customer called in to customer service and was screaming and cussing at one of our associates, she began crying. Hal happened to be walking by and saw her in tears. He asked her what was wrong. She explained the situation, and Hal immediately took the phone from her. He calmly explained to the person on the other end that the way they were speaking to the young lady was not acceptable and that they were never to speak to anyone at his company that way ever again. Later that day, Hal called a company meeting and told the entire staff that, if anyone ever gets a call like that again, to transfer it directly to him.

In another example, Bill Orme, a long-time salesman with Little Giant, remembers how an accountant for the company wanted to cut costs. "His idea was to take all of the airline miles the salesmen earned and use them to purchase future tickets for business. Well, Hal got wind of this and put his foot down."

"Those salesmen earn those air miles," Hal said. "They are to use those to go on trips with their families."

Ted Hartman, head of marketing at Little Giant, remembers a beautiful exchange between Hal and an employee. "Little Giant had a pretty strict dress code which included no visible tattoos," said Ted. "Those who had them were required to cover them while at work. One woman who worked in customer service covered hers with Band-aids. One day, Hal approached her desk and asked her why she was wearing so many Band-aids. When she told him why, he told her to take them off, and that he loved her just the way she was."

Once when Ted's family stopped at the office, Hal scooped up his young son, showed him around and even gave him a toy Porsche to take home. "Hal just created this atmosphere of generosity," Ted explained.

That applied to every area of the business. According to Ted, "Hal practiced radical candor. You always knew where you stood with Hal. He noticed what you were doing. He praised you when you did well and taught you when you needed direction. Hal wanted people to aspire to be more, and they worked harder for him because they knew he genuinely cared about them."

Integrity and good judgment of character served Hal well, and many of his employees stayed with him 30-plus years, several of whom spent their entire career at Little Giant. These are just some of the examples of who Hal Wing was as a boss and how he valued the people he surrounded himself with.

Mark Washburn, longtime friend and business associate of Hal's, remembers Hal's philosophy on building a strong team. "Hal told me this once, and I have never forgotten it. In fact, I use it to this day." Hal said,

> "To be successful, I know I can't know everything. I know a lot, but I don't know it all. So, what I do is like a wagon wheel. I put myself in the middle, and there are several spokes that go out to the rim. At the end of each of those spokes, I put someone I can trust that has my back and will always watch out for me. That way, when I don't know or need something, I can go to those people that I have surrounded myself with."

Karl Nehring, who was Hal's friend and neighbor in Germany recounts, "Hal could identify people's strengths and weaknesses quickly, and he was careful to put people in positions where they could grow and succeed. Hal did not lead from a distance, instead growing and grooming employees so they elevated through the ranks, sometimes from the bottom to the top."

Case in point is Ryan Moss, current CEO of Little Giant. Ryan was hired at an entry level position. Hal worked with him and groomed him, teaching him along the way. When Ryan's wife became pregnant, Hal gave Ryan the exact amount in a raise that they needed so his wife could stay home with their new baby. "One day, Hal was walking by, stopped and told me he was receiving strong promptings to give me a raise. I don't know how Hal knew, but with that raise and a few of my wife's babysitting jobs here and there, we never missed one dollar of my wife's salary, and she was able to be home raising our kids," said Ryan. "That's who Hal was as a mentor, a boss and a man."

Darius Penrod worked for Hal for 37 years and had this to offer about Hal. "I wouldn't be where I am today without Hal." At one point, Darius went to Hal for financial advice. He was young and had a credit card that he had maxed out. He asked Hal what to do. "Hal explained to me that I was only paying a few dollars in principle each month, so it was going to be hard to pay it off. Hal told me,

"Make a mistake, and learn from it."

"Hal paid that credit card off for me, and I have never had a credit card since."

Hal took Darius under his wing, and the two men would often plow and shovel people out on snowy winter mornings and be quite sneaky about it. A few times, Hal would get stuck and have to have Doc come pull him out, but he never got frustrated or angry about it. He just went on plowing and helping people.

A few times, when things got slow at Little Giant, instead of laying people off, Hal would put people to work at his house. "He always made sure he was taking care of his people," Darius said. "I can remember one Christmas, the company didn't have the money to pay Christmas bonuses, so Hal took out a loan so everyone would have one. That is who he was. Even the newest person there got a bonus."

The way Hal treated employees created fierce loyalty to him. One time, someone accidentally started a fire in the plant.

Instead of evacuating, Darius threw the ladders out the back door, so they wouldn't burn.

On another occasion, a water pipe burst at Hal's house. It was about 11 o'clock at night, so Hal resigned himself to the fact that he would have no water in the morning until he could call and get it fixed. A short time later, Hal looked out the window to see several employees with flashlights and headlamps digging up and fixing the pipe.

Hal set a standard that showed his employees that he cared about them, that they were valued and that they could do more and be more. He modeled the behavior, attitude and work ethic he expected. He was an encourager but also a stickler for detail. He was the example that showed everyone who worked for him that with hard work, persistence and never giving up, anything is possible.

"Treat you employees like a campfire. Don't get so close that you get burned, but don't get too far away that you freeze to death."

Halways:

- Surround yourself with good friends and good business associates.
- Assess people based on their potential and abilities. Don't judge a book by its cover.
- Put people in positions where they can grow and succeed. This means understanding their strengths and weaknesses.
- Let people know you care. Common courtesy and kindness breeds loyalty and respect.
- Be willing to do what you ask others to do.

Hal How-Tos:

How are people treated in your current employment environment? What do you do to make people who work for you or with you feel valued?

How do you think valuing people can impact your role in a positive way?

When discipline or confrontation is necessary, do you face it head-on or avoid it and let the situation drag on? How do you feel like that will impact the rest of the team? What do you think that says about you as a leader?

Who do you surround yourself with? Are they people you can trust and who will have your back? Do you keep people close who can help you improve and grow?

What can you do to make communicating in a difficult situation result in positive actions and outcomes?

"I've upped my performance, now up yours."

– Hal Wing

Hal Wing "The Ladder Man" in his office in Springville, Utah (2004)

CHAPTER EIGHT

You Are Responsible for You: Principles for Your Success

One of the biggest things I learned from my dad is accountability and a no-excuses attitude, not because I heard him talk about it, but because he lived it everyday, all the time. I just happened to have a front row seat.

Mark Washburn summed up my dad in just a few poignant words,

"Hal always put the most in to get the most out of every day and every situation."

The interviews I've done for this book of past employees, business associates, family and friends have been a real blessing for me, and I've heard a few common themes. One of these is that Hal was a force of nature. He was an overcomer, and he was the same person in every situation.

Whether he was talking to the president of a company or an employee on the production floor, Hal treated everyone with equal importance. He listened intently and used his words wisely. That's one of the things Mark recalls that made a huge impression on him. "You never heard Hal swear or talk negatively about anyone, especially his wife. He believed that we are responsible for every word we speak and action we take. In the heat of the moment, something that we say that is negative toward someone else could be the one thing that person always remembers about us. Hal said to me once,

'Don't say things to people they'll never forget.'

After 40 years of being friends with Hal, that is one piece of advice I not only never forgot but that impacted how I speak even today."

This also applied to judging people by their looks. I can recall one time my dad had been baling hay at the farm and came in right from the field to a sales meeting without skipping a beat. Later on, he went into Nordstrom to get my mom some perfume. He told the sales lady what he wanted and asked for the biggest bottle she had. When she brought out the smallest bottle, thinking he couldn't afford the perfume, he pulled out a wad of cash, and the woman was totally shocked. She completely changed her tune and got him the biggest bottle.

My dad always said,

> **"Don't judge a book by its cover. Conversations are key. You can miss out on something great if you prejudge someone. Find out who they are as a person first."**

As I mentioned earlier, Hal grew up an underdog. A scrawny kid with bad skin, Hal never let the teasing dissuade him. Instead, he used the bullies' taunting to fuel his drive to succeed.

Hal knew the combination that would unlock his potential was hard work, commitment, drive, and tenacity. He would often say,

"You are never a loser until you quit."

Terry Penrod, a longtime employee of Little Giant says, "Hal always put the time in to be great." This applied to everything

Hal did. "On one occasion, we went horseback riding. Hal was training this horse, and he started to buck, so Hal jumped off. He was hurt pretty badly, so he asked me to drive him home, which I did. I drove back down to put the horses away, and Hal called me. He told me to come back to the house to get him, so I did. He went back to the stable, got the horse out, mounted and just sat on him. He told me he wanted to let that horse know he could not get away with that. I'm pretty sure Hal had some broken ribs from that fall, but that horse never bucked him like that again."

My dad loved horses. He loved riding them, and he loved just being around them. My dad was at the barn when the farrier came to shoe his horses one day. One of the horses got antsy while getting his feet trimmed, and the farrier kicked him. My dad grabbed the guy, threw him against the wall and told him he better never do anything like that again. Hal would not tolerate mistreatment of any kind. His show of respect and care emanated to everything Hal held dear, and he expected those same standards to be upheld by those around him. His principles of right and wrong were unwavering.

These principles also applied at work. When Terry was young, he asked for some extra work to earn more money, so Hal let him clean the machine shop on the weekends. One particular weekend, time got away from Terry. "Friday night, I played basketball and Saturday I was busy, so I put off cleaning the shop until Sunday morning. Well, Hal stopped in and taught me a valuable lesson. He calmly but sternly explained to me that he did not get where he was by working on Sunday, and that he preferred that I not work on Sunday, either. While I wasn't a church going man until later in life, I respected what Hal meant. I never put off doing the job again."

Hal's pursuit of greatness never overshadowed those around him. He always believed the people around him made him better, and he would say to them,

"You take me to the top of the mountain every day."

"When he came to work in the morning," recalls Mark Washburn, "Hal would always come in the back entrance so he had to walk through the plant. This gave him the opportunity to stop and talk to people as he made his way through the building to his office." "Hal's open-door policy at work welcomed everyone," recalls Terry Penrod. "You could tell him anything, and he would listen."

As focused and dedicated to Little Giant as he was, Hal wasn't one of those people who knew what he wanted to do with his life from an early age. Instead, he relied on his strengths and opportunity to guide him.

Each of us is responsible to do the same. At the end of the day, we are accountable for our own choices and our own lives. Your life is what you make it. If you are in a job where you are unfulfilled, use that experience to help guide you to the next opportunity that is more suited for you. While you're there, make the most of it, and look for ways to benefit by taking full advantage of everything that can help position you for your advancement. Learn from your company, your colleagues and your customers. Every situation is an opportunity for growth, but you are responsible to recognize that and use it to your advantage.

The reality is that no one is going to do it for you. You are responsible for *you*; who you are and what you achieve. In every problem, every challenge and every situation, the common denominator is *you*. Never be a victim or allow yourself to laze through your life. Be purposeful. Take ownership. Put the "Hal Factor" in play for you and show yourself and everyone around you exactly what you are capable of. You get to decide who you are today and who you become—no one else. Your words and your thoughts dictate your future. That is what fueled Hal, and I hope it also will fuel you as it has me.

Here are the opportunities-turned-principles of Hal's that he shares with you to help in your own climb up the ladder of success. As you read through them, think of your own life and what has influenced you so far.

Opportunity number one was his parents' farm. Hal learned the discipline of hard work very early in life and how it reaped great rewards, not only in terms of the harvest but in the ability to help and serve others. Sometimes, we look back at our childhood with disdain or regret. Hal used early experiences and difficult situations as building blocks for his life and career. How can each of us look back and find opportunity in our early life? What can we draw from our past to help us better shape our future?

Opportunity number two was the military. Hal served overseas in Germany, which opened up a whole new world for him. He learned toughness, both mental and physical. He also was exposed, for the first time, to the world beyond his own community. Hal saw that there was so much opportunity beyond what he had known before.

Once we are out on our own is the first time we are really in charge of what we do and how we live. How did this time, or how is that time, being used in your life? What kind of choices are you making? Are you living your life on purpose, or are you only taking opportunities that are presented to you? How can we look beyond what is known and comfortable to actively seek out what may be our greatest opportunity?

Opportunity number three was employment. As a young man with a wife and seven children at home, Hal knew he had to succeed. He had a very profitable job selling life insurance.

Because Hal had served in the military in Germany and spoke the language, his company asked him to relocate to Germany to open an insurance office there. Hal moved his whole family to Germany with him, and they lived there for about three years while the office got established. It was while he was in Germany that he met the gentleman that had the original prototype of the multi-purpose ladder. My dad developed a relationship with Walter Kummerlin, the inventor of the ladder, and when Hal returned to America, he purchased a container. The rest is history. The Little Giant Ladder Company was born.

Opportunity number four was business ownership. Hal returned from Germany with some inventory to sell. Initially, he pre-sold all of the ladders he had shipped from Germany. When most of those sales fell through, Hal went on the road for the first time selling face-to-face in order to move his ladder inventory. That first year in business, Hal sold $500,000 worth of ladders by himself. He then began designing and building hinged ladders in his garage. He put those ladders in the back of our station wagon and went out on the road cold-calling and selling, sleeping in the car and eating packed lunches from my mom.

He grew the company literally not from the ground up but from the garage up. He opened the first shop and manufacturing facility and grew to a larger facility. As the company grew, so did Hal's focus on and commitment to people. He understood the value of the employees, and his genuine goal was for everyone to be as successful as he was. He shared in every aspect of his success.

It was in this season of Hal's life that the previous opportunities, experiences and developed principles began to really show and become visible to those around him.

Opportunity number five was missionary work. By giving and serving others, Hal lived in service to his community. He served his church and people through sharing the blessings and gifts he had been given. Even with a difficult assignment at a church with many challenges, Hal led with heart, compassion and encouragement. My parents' programs were wildly successful and their influence is still felt at that church today. Like so many, the things Hal did for people changed their lives for the better. He made everyone feel special, and people remembered and loved him for it. Years later, when I traveled to Germany with my dad, at every restaurant and shop we went in, Hal was greeted with a warm welcome. Everyone remembered him and was happy to see him.

Opportunity number six was philanthropy. As Hal's wealth grew, so did his belief that he was to share that wealth by helping others. He would say,

> **"The gifts and blessings we have been given are on loan to us. One day, we will be asked to give an account of what we did with what we are given."**

Hal loved his community and took it upon himself to care for it and its citizens in a way that sometimes only he knew. Whether it was a need in the police department, a resident who needed a new roof, or an employee who needed a reliable car, Hal was there with support and resources. Almost every time, it was anonymous. Hal was not interested in recognition or reward, he was simply dedicated to helping others. He was committed to blessing others the way he was blessed.

Hal did things with heart, and he was an intentional person. When you have heart, you execute in a way that others don't. For Hal, success wasn't just about *hard* work, it also was about *heart* work.

Hal always wanted to make a difference, and he did for so many. How he lived his life and the things he did left a mark on every person he knew and every person he touched. That is a life beyond legacy.

Halways:

- How can you use your past experiences to help build your future, to help you determine what you do want instead of what you don't want?
- How can you use Hal's opportunities and actions to help you build your own principles of success?
- At the heart of every aspect of Hal's life was his dedication to and his value of people. Can you say the same? How do you view and treat those around you—your colleagues, your employees, your friends and your neighbors? How can you begin to take that same approach to success?

Hal How-Tos:

Go about your day with intention. Know what you want to achieve and stay focused on your goals.

Act with integrity and treat others in a way that lifts them up in every situation.

Assess your life experiences from childhood on. What can you take from those experiences that can serve you well today and into the future?

"I don't know why they call it cold hard cash. I've always thought that it was warm and soft."

– Hal Wing

Hal Wing with one of his collector cars (2008)

CHAPTER NINE
Take the Risk, Not the Regret

At the height of the timing of the knock-off products, Little Giant was really trying to break through the barrier and grow. We were coming off of some challenging sales cycles, and we needed some wind in our sales. Hal was known to be an innovator and a risk taker, but I had no idea what he was about to take on and how it could possibly pay off.

We had all seen infomercials by that time, those late night and Saturday morning shows with high pitched yelling hosts hawking everything from cookware to cleaning products.

Hal had an idea, and he knew what he wanted the end game to be. Even though no hardware product like ours had ever done it, Hal thought the infomercial could get us there and open us up to a whole new customer base with direct-to-consumer advertising. The challenge was how to pay for it. The cost was one million dollars.

Hal leveraged his farm (the land I told you earlier he donated to the church for the chapels) to pay for that infomercial. Once he signed on the dotted line, it was go time. Hal was a planner but bet it all on the potential of Little Giant. He believed that we should

"Prepare for the worst, and work as if all things will work out for the best."

When he met with Doug Fowkes of Infomercials, Inc. Doug knew he had a winner on his hands right away. "Hal was a bigger-than-life personality, and he had that It Factor," he said. "I called it The Hal. We knew right away he had to host the infomercial because there was no way we could ever find anyone who was more passionate about those ladders than Hal."

Robin Hartl Trout agreed. "Hal had very specific goals for this program. He followed very specific steps. If anything got in his way, he just rerouted around it."

One of those reroutings was the script. Hal was given a huge script to learn and recite. One go with that, and he literally threw it down and said, "No. I am going to do this my way. I don't need a script, and I don't want a script." From that point on, Hal winged it (pun intended), and it was pure magic.

Brandon Moss was on set as Hal's right hand and ladder wrangler. "Hal was amazing. One time, he even did the infomercial with severe injuries from a crash, and you would never know it. Between takes he would lay down, but once those cameras rolled, he was on." Brandon went on to explain why he thinks the infomercial was such a success for Little Giant. "Hal was just so genuine and passionate. He knew everything about his product, and he believed in it. Those things alone made people trust him and want to buy his ladders. Even today, people see the infomercial and probably don't even know Hal has passed away. The fact that this program continues to run successfully today after all of these years is incredible. In fact, we still have a call center in Toledo that takes infomercial orders."

With high hopes, the first infomercial airing led to initial disappointment. Only four calls were received and one sale recorded. This turned out to be a test run. "What the production company told us was not that we only had one sale, it was that we had a 25% conversion rate, and that was unheard of with infomercials," Brandon said. "There was some tweaking after that, and things took off from there. The phones went crazy. We went from making 400 ladders a day to 7,000 a day in a very short time."

The infomercial grew to huge success and sell out numbers. The plant had to hire a bunch of people and began working three shifts to accommodate all of the new orders.

In the midst of all of this, Home Depot contacted us and told us that people were going into their stores, asking for Little Giant ladders, so they wanted to carry them. That led to Bed, Bath and Beyond, Target and even Linens 'n' Things contacting us wanting to carry our ladders. You could find Little Giant in so many places so quickly. It literally changed everything. The company was able to pay cash for machines and upgrade systems.

"The Little Giant infomercial really launched us, too," said Fowkes. Sales tripled for Infomercials, Inc. literally overnight. "It changed not only their business, but our business and the marketing industry as a whole," he added. Everyone wanted to get in on the infomercial success that Little Giant had found. All of this was because Hal took a risk and never let anything get in his way.

By the end of that year, the company had grown four times its size because of the infomercial. It grew four times larger again the following year. Hal knew he could never have accomplished what he had was it not for his team of employees, in every department, on every shift. So, Hal went out on a limb again. One day, I was in a management meeting with our CEO, CFO and my brother. My dad walked in and said, "I want to give back to our employees for all of their hard work getting us here. Can we do it?" The CFO said he would run the numbers but cautioned Hal that there was a lot of money in play. Was he sure he wanted to do it? Hal confidently shot back,

"If we can do it, I am going to do it."

Once all was a go, the management team at Little Giant put together a list of all of the employees by name, years of service and position. It was then determined how much of a bonus all three hundred employees would receive. Finally, the day came that we were going to announce the bonuses.

Hal came into the manufacturing lunchroom and made the announcement. First, the employees started screaming, yelling and clapping.

Then, as the checks were personally handed out by Hal, there were hugs and many tears shed. I was so proud of my dad's generosity as one by one the employees came through and received their bonus checks.

We could have placed these bonuses in their regular paychecks along with a letter to them, but my dad wanted to thank and recognize his amazing employees personally. It was an honor to stand next to my dad as employees hugged us as they picked up their bonuses. One lesson I learned that day was,

"People are more important than things."

That day, my dad distributed one million dollars to his employees. Even the very newest employees received a bonus check.

My dad developed a great team, and that great team developed a superior product. Now that product, thanks in large part to the infomercial, was more well-known and selling better than ever.

The key questions and principles upon which the product lines were developed and marketed through the infomercial remain the same principles upon which Little Giant products are developed today:

1. Are they safer?
2. Are they more efficient?
3. Does it make someone's job easier?
4. Does it provide a good experience for the user?

To date, this infomercial is the most successful one ever in the hardware category. The shelf life of an infomercial is usually no longer than 24 months. The Little Giant Ladder infomercial is still running and selling ladders today. You may even catch Hal on TV giving his award-winning performance and dynamite demonstration.

After risking everything, the payoff was the ultimate redemption. The company was growing and thriving, the employees were growing and thriving and my dad was at the center of it all, risking everything on a Wing and a prayer.

*Hal*ways:

- How much confidence and faith do you have in yourself to take risks?
- How do you determine what is a strategic risk? If it pays off, how would you be rewarded?
- When it comes to moving forward, how willing are you to take steps and actions needed to get you to the next level?

Hal How-Tos:

Think about your current role or position. What can you do to begin to plan your next move? How can you add value? How can you think outside the box and take risks that can pay off big for you?

Determine what and who you need to help you take actions to get ahead and grow. While it's not always comfortable, sometimes we have to get outside our comfort zone to reach our full potential.

Make a list of possible things you can do in your current situation that would get you closer to doing or being exactly what you dream.

"Let's get going. We're burning daylight."

– Hal Wing

Hal Wing at an off-road motorcycle race in central Utah (1980)

CHAPTER TEN
Actions Speak Louder

"The faster Hal went, the happier he was," recalls Scott Finlayson. That was true in every aspect of Hal's life. He embraced life with vigor and a wide open throttle. Whether it was running the business, riding dirt bikes or driving fast cars, Hal was all in, all the time.

It was this quest for achievement that I think made him so driven and ultimately so successful. Literally, you could not keep the man down. Sometimes, he didn't even take time to eat.

I can remember once my brother and I went on a Harley ride with him. As we pulled into a service station, Hal pulled up to stop and passed out. He and his bike went crashing to the ground. My brother and I and two farmers picked him up and carried him into the convenience store. When Hal came to, he asked about his bike. We tried to calm him down and told him the bike could be repaired but that the tank got smashed. Shortly after, the paramedics arrived, and they started asking him questions.

One of the paramedics asked, "Hal, when was the last time you ate something?" Hal answered, "Oh, about two days ago." The paramedic was shocked. "What is going on, Hal?" My dad laughed and said, "I'm just busy having too much fun. I haven't had time to eat." Ultimately, my dad was fine that day, but his blood sugar had bottomed out. Once we got some food in him, he was back on his bike flying down the road.

Chris Holmes, a former salesman for Little Giant remembers Hal this way, "Everything Hal did, he did all the way." That was certainly true. Someone once said he thought my dad had 900 lives, and now looking back, I think he might be right.

My dad approached everything with a "go" mindset. He was never afraid and believed in giving it 100%, sometimes much to the dismay of himself or his passengers.

"One time," says Holmes, "a news crew was coming to tape a segment at the plant. Hal was on his motorcycle, revved it and wiped out on the wet grass. The force of the fall embedded Hal's sunglasses into his forehead and blood was gushing everywhere. The reporter passed out, and Hal went to the hospital."

In another instance, Hal came huffing into the office. He told me he was going 90 mph on Main Street, and the police were looking for him. That was one of the few days *I* got to lecture *him*.

Terry Penrod remembers his first meeting with Hal. At my parents' annual summer company party, The Summer Hummer, Terry, who was new to the company, had won a trip to go with Hal and some other employees to Lake Powell to go water skiing. (Hal often took employees on these trips as rewards or just fun getaways.) As Terry remembers, "Hal was a mad-man skier. He would go fast and try to get as close to the rocks as possible to spray them."

He also recalls driving Hal's Solstice. Hal purchased the car at the annual SEMA show in Las Vegas. It was a concept car and one of a kind. The car had a Nascar racing engine in it with over 1,000 horsepower. It was never intended to be driven on the street; that is until Hal got hold of it. Somehow, my dad was able to get it licensed and registered in the state of Utah. Hal asked Terry to bring the car to him at his winter home in St. George, Utah. Terry drove the car to him, they unloaded it, and Hal got in the driver's seat. When Terry heard a click, he realized that Hal put on his seatbelt. He had never known Hal to wear one. In a split second, they were sideways and Terry was grasping for his seatbelt. "That car was scary fast, and Hal loved every minute of it."

Terry helped my dad with a lot of special projects, so he got to know my dad really well. Once when he and my dad were making a pheasant run, Terry accidentally hit my dad with a pipe and knocked him out cold. Another time, they were painting my dad's house and Hal fell off the scaffolding. Terry called the squad who came quickly. One of the paramedics who was working on Hal called out, "Is there a Terry here?" Terry walked over, leaned down to Hal, who quietly said, "Finish the job, Terry." That was Hal, no matter what, he got back up, and he finished the job.

Mark Washburn and his brother owned the local Nissan dealership. When Mark got the new 300ZX in stock, he called Hal right away. He drove it over and picked up Hal at the plant, so he could take it for a spin. Hal clearly had his favorite roads, and they ended up on a windy stretch that ran alongside a railroad track. Before Mark knew what was happening, Hal had it going over 100 mph. As they entered an S-curve, the back end started to swing out sideways. Hal knew what he was doing and pulled the car back around. "Now, this car only had 10 miles on it when I took it over to Hal, and I was thinking I just needed to hang on for dear life and hope the car and I would survive."

On another trip, Mark went snowmobiling with Hal. Once again, Hal was in open throttle mode with the machine going over 100 mph. Hal was having a blast banking up and down the drifts until he hit something. Hal flew off the snowmobile, and it rolled about eight times. Hal got up, flipped it over, got right back on and away they went.

Hal liked to go dirt bike riding on Friday mornings with whomever was up for a ride. On one occasion, Mark's son Caleb offered to go. About 1 PM, Hal called Mark and told him that Caleb had wiped out, but that he thought he was okay. Hal had driven him to the local hospital and left him there because he had a meeting at the office. Mark knew Hal had left Caleb in capable hands, and sure enough, Caleb was fine. It was tough hanging with Hal, though. It didn't matter if you were young or old, in cars, on skis or dirt bikes, Hal Wing was out to win and willing to go all out to do it.

As you know, Hal enjoyed riding horses. Not just any horses; he loved the Arabian breed. He liked horses with spirit that were challenging to break. One day, he was out horse shopping at the Taylor Ranch in Utah. The owner of the ranch was showing him several horses. He would point to a horse and say, "That would be a nice horse for you, Hal." My dad saw a beautiful horse and asked, "What about that horse?" The owner of the ranch told him, "That horse will never be ridden by anyone." Hal looked at him and said, "I'll take that horse." That horse was named Sickle and was his all time favorite horse. There's a picture of my dad and Sickle at the beginning of the next chapter.

When my dad was in his sixties, he began to get serious about fitness and weight training. He even went out and purchased all of the best equipment for his home gym. One day, he called me and told me how sore he was. In fact, he said he was so sore he could barely walk. I asked him, "Dad, how long are your workouts?" He replied, "Well, they're about three to four hours long, and I keep track of all of the weight I lift each week." It was some crazy number of pounds he was lifting each week. I had to explain to him that his workout should last about 45 minutes. Anything over that would actually be hurting his muscles more than building them. That was Hal, though, going all in and doing everything 110%.

The same was true in business. Hal was a man of action. He was full of life and full of qualities that made him unique and destined to succeed.

Here are 10 core qualities that set Hal apart from the world:

1. Hal was willing to take risks. He assessed the opportunity and bet on himself, his company and his employees to win every time.

2. Hal was willing to do whatever it took to make it happen, even when that meant sleeping in his car on top of ladders more than 300 days a year.

3. Hal looked at his competition as second place. He knew his value and never wavered from his belief in his product and in his people.

4. He constantly improved himself and his business by thinking outside the box and taking action every day toward his goals.

5. He gave without expectation. He genuinely wanted to help people and wanted nothing, not even recognition, in return.

6. The only thing he measured with was a tape measure. He believed in people. He gave people chances and set them up for success.

7. He was a man of action and spent little time contemplating. He made decisions and moved forward.

8. He understood the value of people.

9. He went out of his way to help all people, whoever needed help.

10. He used the Wing Formula: quality + value (not price) = profit

No matter what my dad did, he did it with 100% confidence and assertion. If he was going to win, he was going to win big. If he was going to crash, he was going to crash big. In fact, he did both. I can remember stories of my dad crashing many dirt bikes. They knew him at the hospital and were never surprised when he ended up there. On more than one occasion, though, Hal had someone waiting with a truck outside to pull around so he could break himself out of the hospital, jump in the truck and speed off for home. His was a life of constant adventure and fulfillment on so many levels.

What I have learned from my dad is to take whatever passion that is deep inside of you and find a way to channel your energy and take action to make it your reality. For my dad, those passions were family, ladders, helping people, and fast machines. Whatever he did, he left it all on the field. In the end, he had no regrets, a lifetime of experiences, a thriving business and countless lives touched. What more can any of us ask for?

Halways:

- At what speed do you operate every day?
- Are you focused on a goal or passion?
- Are you self-motivated to achieve your dreams?
- What actions are you taking to improve or reach your goals?
- Do you talk about what you want, or do you take actions to actually achieve or attain what you want?

Hal How-Tos:

Really think about what you are passionate about. Write it down. Now identify what you can do to make that passion your career or part of your everyday life.

What actions can you take today and each day to get you closer to living your passion? List them out on paper. How can you use the position you are currently in to help identify your calling or get you closer to your goal?

Every experience helps us advance in some way. Look for ways in your current career path or position that can help you improve in an area in which you can benefit.

Give 100% at your job or in your business. Approach every situation the way Hal did. Put the most in, so you can get the most out of every day.

"None of the THINGS we have will be worth a gust of air 100 years from now! It will matter, however, how we treat each other, what we say, how we act, and what we think – of this I am certain!!!!"

– Hal Wing

Hal Wing on his favorite horse Sickle at the Little Sahara Sand Dunes in Utah (1997)

CHAPTER ELEVEN
Change Starts with Me

As fast as Hal moved all the time, he never missed a beat. To say that Hal was observant was an understatement. Somehow, he always seemed to know the needs of those in our community, and he never missed an opportunity to step up and help.

Doc Shell, Hal's very first employee, stayed with Hal his entire career. In fact, Doc could build a ladder all by himself. Later in his career, Doc took on the role of doing special projects for Hal. "I would drive around with gas in the back of my truck. Whenever I came across someone who had run out of gas, I would fill their tank."

Dave Francis, Doug's cousin who has worked at Little Giant since 1982, said that, more than 50 times, he delivered envelopes to people on behalf of Hal. Even though he worked in the plant, he kept a dress shirt in his car in case he was sent on a mission by Hal.

Shortly after Steve Curtis was hired, he remembers receiving a phone call from Hal asking Steve to meet him at an address in town. When Steve arrived, Hal was there waiting. Hal said, "Steve, look at the roof on this house. It needs to be replaced. Please go knock on the door and tell them that someone will be replacing their roof, but please do not give them my name." Steve was scared to knock on the door, but he did it. When the homeowner came to the door, Steve told him that someone would be coming to replace his roof. The homeowner was very perplexed, but after a few minutes said thank you. Shortly after, the roof was replaced.

On another occasion, Steve remembers receiving a phone call from Hal asking to again meet him at another address. When Steve arrived, Hal said, "Look at the tires on this car. They need new tires. Please knock on the door and tell them to go to Johnson Tire on Main Street, and their tires will be replaced. Please don't use my name." The tires were replaced.

Speaking of tires, Karl Nehring, who lived down the street from Hal when he was in Germany selling insurance, tells the story of Hal putting tires on his car when he could not afford them himself. "Hal was always looking for an opportunity to help and be of service to others. He is one of the most influential people in my life. I learned so much about how important it is to value people and cherish relationships. Hal was one of a kind."

What says so much about Hal is the friendships he built and kept throughout his life. Earhardt Beuttenmuller served in the military in Germany with Hal and remembers the two changing oil together so they could save money. When Earhardt got married, he remembers his friend coming to his aid. "When my wife and I got married, we had to do a courthouse wedding first before we could be married in the church. We were in a spot, though, because of the documents we needed and the language barrier. All of a sudden, Hal showed up at the courthouse and translated all the documents for us right then and there so we could have our wedding."

While the two were in Germany, Earhardt made lamps and shades and gave his best one to Hal, and Hal never forgot it. Years later, Earhardt once asked Hal why they were friends, and Hal quickly replied, "You taught me how to be generous."

Back in the U.S., the two men continued to be best friends. Once when Earhardt was moving from Colorado to Georgia, the moving van burned with all of his and his family's belongings in it. Hal sent him a check for $5,000. "What was so incredible was that, although I didn't know it at the time, Hal took out a loan to give me that money," said Earhardt. "The company was not doing well at that time, but Hal helped me anyway."

Once, when Earhardt was visiting Hal at Christmastime, he got to see how loved Hal was by his employees. Hal had just given out Christmas bonuses, and when he and Earhardt walked into the lunch room, everyone stood up and clapped for Hal. "He was loved by everyone," remembers Earhardt.

The stories go on and on. Ted Hartman lived next door to a kind woman who became a surrogate mother to him and his wife. It so happens that she was married to a distant cousin of Hal's. When he passed away, Hal learned that his wife's green card was being revoked, and she was going to be deported, along with her son. After being in this country for so long, all of her family was here. It was an incredibly stressful situation.

At the office one morning, Hal said he wanted to see Ted. He invited Ted up to the house so they could talk. My dad and mom talked with Ted about how they could help. The woman did not have much money, so Hal told him they would fund the process for her stay in the United States.

Over the course of the next several months, Ted took ten trips to Salt Lake City and spent thousands of hours helping her. She got a green card, and Ted helped her study for her citizenship test. She passed with flying colors and became a citizen. "All that time I spent," said Ted, "and Hal never said a word to me about it. This could've never happened without Hal and Brigitte's help. If it weren't for Hal, she would've surely been deported."

Hal was quite visible in the community. He wasn't just known as the Little Giant Ladder man. He also was the giant-sized candy man. Hal loved Halloween. Every year, he would dress up in costume and take giant sized candy bars to the office and down to Main Street where he would hand them out to all the kids trick-or-treating. To this day, someone hands out giant sized candy bars on Main Street every Halloween in honor of Hal Wing.

Hal would often ride his horse all over town. One day, Hal rode in and hitched Sickle up at the local drive-in restaurant. "I remember it like it was yesterday," said Mike O'Reilly. "Hal was decked out in full leather chaps and everything. Here are all these cars, parked at the speakers, and this guy hitches up his horse. So, I went out to meet him. I introduced myself, and he promptly ordered two large vanilla ice cream cones. I went and got the cones, and he proceeded to eat one and give the other to his horse. We started chatting, and he noticed the poster in the window. My son had leukemia, and we were doing a fundraiser so he could have a bone marrow transplant. Hal asked me about it, so I told him all about my son. As we talked, he pulled a bundle of cash out of his pocket and handed it to me. It was $5,000. He told me he wanted to donate it toward the fundraiser for my son. That day, Hal Wing became my best friend."

Years later, when Mike closed down his restaurant, where do you think he went to work? That's right, Little Giant. He was a longtime member of our team.

Don Livingstone, an advisor and on the first board at Little Giant, first met Hal on the driving range. Hal gave him a Little Giant putter. "I used that putter for 20 years until it broke," Don recalled fondly.

Don ran the entrepreneurship program at Brigham Young University. He invited Hal to come speak. Don's nephew from Alberta was staying with him at the time, and the young man attended the event. "During his presentation, Hal did a demonstration for the class where he climbed to the top of a ladder and yodeled," recalls Don. "It made quite the impression." Afterward, Don introduced Hal to his nephew. When Hal learned that he was preparing to go on a mission with the church, Hal gave him a sizable sponsorship check. "It was such a kind gesture of support for someone Hal had just met but who was in alignment with his faith and values," said Don.

The two men struck up a friendship. Hal asked Don to advise him, so he did and served on the board of Little Giant until he left for a church mission in Africa.

In August of 2006, the irrigation canal behind Mel Huffaker's house breached and flooded his home for more than 32 days. A small flood for a day or two can easily be cleaned without any long-term effects, but when the water flows for 32 days straight, mold grows and makes the home uninhabitable. The irrigation company was unwilling to shut the water off for a couple of days to fix the canal because of some big farms that wanted the water. Due to the mold, the Huffakers ended up leaving home for what ended up being nearly five years, while they litigated with the insurance company.

When word got out at work that Mel's home was flooded and they had to move out, Hal called Mel into his office and said, "Mel, we understand your home was flooded, and we would like to help. We would like to hire an attorney to help you with your case." I thanked him for his generosity but said we had already hired an attorney. It was very kind of him to offer, and looking back on the final outcome, I wished I would have taken him up on the offer."

Years passed as the attorneys for the other side stalled and delayed, hoping that if they could drag it out, the Huffakers would cave in and go away. After the fourth year of making regular house payments on a house they couldn't live in, and making the monthly payments on a rental, money was getting tight. Mel had spent over $100,000 on the case.

Mel struggled with the stress of the whole situation, not knowing how to pay another month of rent plus the mortgage. His situation weighing heavy on his mind, Mel was walking down the hall at work one day when Hal happened to be walking in the opposite direction. He stopped Mel in the hall and asked how things were going with his home. Mel explained that the attorneys for the other side were stalling and hoping he would drop the case. Just then, Hal reached into his pocket and pulled out a check for $10,000 with Mel's name already filled out and said, "Take this check; it will help you fight a little longer." Mel was not a very emotional man, but tears filled his eyes because this could not have come at a more dire time for him and his family. Hal saw his emotional state, hugged him and said, "Mel, don't give up."

That money helped the Huffakers survive for another eight months until the trial. To this day, he doesn't know how Hal knew that he had hit his low point, but he did, and it was a blessing.

"Over the 25 years I worked at Wing Enterprises, I can't tell you how many people have said to me [once they knew I worked for Hal], let me tell you about my experience with Hal Wing," said Mel. "I've had several people tell me that their car broke down, and he bought them a new car. I even had an older woman tell me that he bought her a house. Hal would ask these people that he helped not to tell anyone. But after he passed, most felt it was okay to share with others the generosity of this great man. Hal was indeed a blessing in the lives of so many people, including me," he added. "Hal understood the savior's decree to the world,

> **"Inasmuch as ye have done it unto one of the least of these my brethren, ye have done it unto me." Matthew 25:40**

Hal not only gave of his time and talents, but he also gave of himself. Nikki Allen, Hal's assistant, recalls him coming to her wedding. "It was shortly after Hal's accident, and he surprised me by coming to my wedding. He was in one of those jazzy chairs, and he was white as a ghost. He wasn't even strong enough to walk. I know Brigitte did not want him to come, but he was bound and determined to be there for me on my wedding day. That was just who Hal was. While on my honeymoon, I received a call from my brother telling me that Hal was in the hospital. He passed away a few days later. I have often thought to myself how lucky I was to have worked for Hal and got to see him in action every day. Everything here at Little Giant is because of Hal. I am so thankful I had a boss I loved so much and who thought so much of me."

Halways:

- How observant are you to the people and situations around you?
- Do you look for ways to be of help?
- Are you willing and able to put yourself in someone else's shoes?
- Are you sharing what you have with others?

Hal How-Tos:

When I ask if you are sharing what you have with others, this doesn't necessarily mean material things. Sure, that is nice. But, think about other things. What talents, experience, stories or skills of yours can you share that might help or encourage someone around you?

Look for ways to take this same principle and apply it to your customers. How can you be of service to them? How can you make their experience with you and at your place of business exceptional?

Think of ways you can be generous that don't involve money. Kindness, consideration and guidance are all great examples of ways we can be generous toward others. Put this into play today. You'll be amazed at what you receive in return.

"The harder I work, the luckier I get."

– Hal Wing

Hal Wing on the set of the infomercial (2003)

CHAPTER TWELVE
Selling Innovation

I had the benefit of leading the sales department for a good portion of my career. Knowing how my dad valued the sales team, it made me proud that I was able to carry on his attention to detail and commitment to the customer in every Little Giant transaction. Being out on the road, doing shows (sometimes even with Hal) and visiting customers the way he did brought me great joy.

I had some big shoes to fill, though. My dad set a pretty high standard, and I did not take that lightly. I learned all I could from him from the time I started cleaning the bathrooms at age ten, to building ladders, to attending trade shows with my dad. I soaked in every bit of wisdom I could get.

When it became my turn to join and eventually lead the sales team, I did so with the same dedication to quality, honesty and integrity upon which my dad built the company. He saw this and always made sure I knew he was there to help and support me.

Things were really fun once the infomercial was humming along. We would go to trade shows, and I would be demonstrating a ladder to a guy, trying to convince him to buy. Then, along came another guy who looked at the ladder, then at the first man and said, "I bought one of these about nine years ago. Best purchase I ever made." And just like that...sold. Now, that didn't happen every time, but it happened a lot. All because of the commitment to quality my dad demanded and bet the farm on (literally) so many years ago.

Hal was creative and all about innovation from the very beginning. Even when he brought the first ladder design back to America, he was thinking about it, troubleshooting it and enhancing the design. In fact, he changed and improved the ladder so much, the original company in Germany purchased parts from Little Giant.

After the company had achieved massive growth as a result of the infomercial, word was out in the industry that Little Giant was the place to be for those in the business. Scott and Kathy Patton know this well. They both came from Werner Ladder. Scott recalls how when Hal brought him to Utah to interview, he spent the whole day with Scott. "I was just in awe of how Hal dedicated his entire day to me," said Scott. "He took me around and introduced me, both in the office and in the plant. He literally knew everyone's name. It was so impressive." When Scott accepted a position at Little Giant, he and his wife Kathy made the move to Utah. They both came to work for us and have been with us ever since.

"Hal had the mentality that we could do anything as a company, and that no challenge or idea was too big," recalls Kathy. "That energy was infectious and encouraged the employees to be creative and provide input and suggestions. We all felt valued, along with an overwhelming sense of family."

According to Scott, "Hal was the hardest worker I ever knew." He remembers Hal saying,

"Once you've sold a ladder, you've only just begun."

Selling the ladder was just the tip of the iceberg. From there, it was identifying what else the customer needed or could use and then selling them additional enhancements that made that sale customized for each individual. "Hal was larger than life, and he always made you feel like you wanted to do your very best for him," shared Kathy.

Hal would teach closing techniques regularly in weekly sales meetings. In addition to the up-sell I mentioned above, Hal was always training the sales team. "It starts with attitude," Hal would say,

> ## "Sometimes, we all need a check up from the neck up."

I think that came from his start in the insurance business. My dad had plenty of doors slammed in his face while selling insurance. That led him to having thick skin and a "Thank you…next!" mentality when it came to sales. He would tell us,

> ## "Don't take 'no' personally. They obviously have a problem, so go find someone who doesn't have a problem. It's that simple."

Wherever you are in your career and whatever you do, always remember that you are in sales. It is a fundamental principle of business and life. The art of persuasion is a skill that those who master will reap great rewards. My father is a perfect example of someone who mastered the art of sales by continually working and striving for excellence in all areas of business and life. As a result of those efforts, he built a fiercely loyal team, an international powerhouse brand and a whole new category of ladder. The customers followed and helped make Little Giant the household name it is today.

We are proud to have such raving fans as customers. Here is one such story we received from a customer. This man was on the job, driving a utility van and had a Little Giant ladder directly behind his driver's seat. He fell asleep at the wheel, and the van rolled multiple times. The ladder acted as a roll cage and ended up saving his life. While one of our guiding principles is developing products that are safe, we could've never imagined that our ladder would provide that type of safety. These are the types of stories we hear often, and we are so proud of each and every one.

Hal was always innovating, and he encouraged everyone at the company to do the same. While our core products were ladders, we dabbled in creating other products to sell. Ryan Moss, our current CEO, actually holds the most Little Giant patents to date. When Ryan created a hitch design, the company developed and sold them for a few years. They ended up being so successful, a company in Kansas City bought the whole business unit.

I am proud to say that each year, Little Giant applies for more patents than all the other ladder companies combined. Does that surprise you? It shouldn't. Little Giant now has between 50 and 70 SKUs in our product assortment across categories. Because of Hal, we continue to innovate, grow and thrive as a company today. His dream of a legacy business is realized.

The company has benefited many times over from the investment Hal made in the infomercial. A program that was supposed to have a shelf life of two years has now been running since 2003. That success has led to significant investment in the company, specifically innovation.

One of these investments in innovation led to the development of a fiberglass ladder line now sold at Lowe's. When we could not source enough quality fiberglass from a domestic manufacturer, we decided to make our own. Led by Ryan Moss, we learned everything we needed to know, designed all the machines ourselves, made the space and started the production line. It paid off.

In the last five years at Little Giant, we have sold more than $150 million in ladders to the cable industry. This industry has been my personal baby, and I am so proud, not only of the innovation and safety we provide but in pure Hal fashion, the opportunities that have come and the careers that have opened up.

Along the way, we also did some special projects and promotional programs. For example, we created a special version of the Little Giant ladder for QVC that was a little lighter and a lower price point. The result was astounding. We sold 25,000 ladders in 24 hours. Yes, you read that right. That is more than 1,000 ladders an hour. It was a Christmas promotion, and it could not have gone better. It was this type of out-of-the-box thinking, innovation and sales focus that helped us not only grow but expand our revenue streams. Using Hal's principles and taking action, we were able to continue to evolve and grow the company at great speed.

As we talk specifically about sales and innovation, it also is important to discuss the power of the brand. Because of the company's long history and solid reputation, the name Little Giant was synonymous with quality and integrity, thanks solely to Hal, his vision and his dedication.

Once we began airing the infomercial, Little Giant the brand was introduced to millions of households all over the U.S. and the world. Today, Little Giant is the most well-known and the most popular ladder brand in the world. Are we the cheapest? No. That is an important answer, and the key to a powerful brand strategy. Because our focus was always consistent quality and attention to detail, our foundation was laid and built upon solidly. As we began to market and grow, that foundation served us well, both from a grassroots perspective at events like trade shows and also on a grander scale on television through the infomercial hosted by Hal.

We know that the power of the brand is strong. Brand beats price—but quality beats brand. Because Hal built our company the way he did, our brand presence today makes us not only the best, but the most popular in the world.

Halways:

- In what ways are you connecting with customers in your sales process?
- Are you focused on just making a sale or providing customers a product or products they need?
- How can you innovate in your current role?
- Do you have ideas for ways to improve or create new products? Do you bring those ideas to anyone's attention?
- How can you think outside the box to improve your sales or increase your average ticket?
- How can you become more valuable to your employer by innovating on the job?

Hal How-Tos:

When you are on the sales floor, what is on your mind? Do you actively seek out customers to help? If not, try doing that on your next shift. Ask them questions to see what they need and how you can help them. See if they buy more as a result. Remember, to the customer, you are the expert. Earn that title.

Do you know the products you sell inside and out? If not, take time out of your day to really learn about the products, how they work and their various applications. Knowing these things will help improve your sales. Also take time to get to know where things are outside your designated department. Not only does this make you more valuable, it will help improve your units per transaction.

"If it's not a good deal for everyone at the table, it's not a good deal."

– Hal Wing

Hal Wing racing a sprinter on his dirt bike at the announcement of the new Hal Wing Track and Field facility at Utah Valley University (2009)

CHAPTER THIRTEEN
Culture of Community

At this point, you might be thinking that Hal Wing and the rise of the Little Giant Ladder company is an anomaly. On some levels, I could agree with that. My father was a force of nature. I've heard it over and over again, and it is sprinkled throughout this book in each of the stories, examples and situations I have shared with you. Whether it was in his personal life, in the church or at the company, my father loved and believed in people. It was this love and belief that helped make him and our company successful.

After my father passed away, he was inducted into the Pillar of The Valley, a hall of fame type group honoring those who made the biggest impact in the region. At this ceremony, the governor of Utah spoke. I'll never forget his words,

"Hal Wing always said he was in the ladder business, but that wasn't true. Hal was in the people business, and the people built the ladders."

Many of the people I interviewed for this book were with Hal from the very beginning. Many of our employees today came on board early when the company was just starting. Several never had another boss besides Hal, and many of them were emotional recalling working for Hal and the many examples of leadership, collaboration, generosity, fairness and kindness.

At Little Giant, every person was valued and appreciated for their talents and their contributions. But it didn't stop there. Hal knew that the people actually building the ladders, working the machines and talking to the customers were the heart and soul of the company. They were the ones on the front lines, and they also would be the ones who would have ideas on how to make our processes and systems better.

Just as Hal and his first employee, Doc, literally had to be both innovative and creative to figure out how to build the first machines to make the ladders, Hal knew this same mindset would be necessary as the company grew. So, he started the Good Idea Program.

Everyone in the company was encouraged to submit ideas for how to do their jobs better, how to make our processes better, how to make our systems better, how to better communicate, how to more efficiently produce ladders, and on and on. There was nothing off the table, and there was everything to gain.

Hal was the type who would always recognize and praise people in public, and redirect or reprimand them in private. Hal loved this program and gave praise for all of the good ideas people brought to him. He implemented many of them over the years, and those ideas ended up saving the company millions of dollars. All of it because Hal believed in his people and their ability to play a personal role in the success of the company over and above what their day-to-day jobs actually were.

Hal believed in the power of the human spirit, and he was wise in the ways of people. Every morning, as he entered the back door of the business and walked through the manufacturing facility, he stopped to greet and talk with every person he encountered. He took the time to get to know the people who worked for him, which, in turn, allowed him to direct them in ways that they not only could make the greatest contributions to the company, but also would feel the most fulfilled and valued.

On many occasions, Hal used employees to deliver checks, make deliveries and implement good deeds for members of the community that needed help. These types of special missions not only impacted the individual, it also impacted the way that person did their job, how they felt about the company and the impact they were collectively having on the community.

It is a powerful force in business to have everyone bought in and invested in such a way that they understand the impact they make every day is a game changer.

At Little Giant, everyone understood their mission and felt like they were part of the team that made the company successful. Our culture was a family environment that fostered mutual respect, new ideas, clean language, service to others, and commitment to producing a quality product.

Today and every day, those of us who knew Hal, worked for Hal, was the recipient of an anonymous Hal gift, or those who continue to work at Little Giant reap the benefits of the sacrifice, dedication, ingenuity, perseverance, grit and generosity that was the life of Hal Wing and is the spirit of Little Giant still today.

"Hal planted a lot of trees, and we get to enjoy the shade."

— Ryan Moss, CEO
The Little Giant Ladder Company

Halways:

- Do you feel like you are part of a winning team? How can you create that environment in your own organization?
- Do you foster new ideas, ways of looking at situations and doing things differently?
- Do you ever step outside your box to help someone else in your community?

Hal How-Tos:

What are some ways you or your co-workers can work together to generate new ideas for the company? Make a list.

Do you have ideas that could help your company be more efficient, save time or money? If so, write it up and submit it to your boss. If not, look for ways to innovate. A company is never too big to implement even the smallest ideas if they can impact the bottom line.

Develop and pitch some type of reward system at your place of work that fosters creativity and gets buy-in from all of the employees. Use Hal's program as your starting point.

Get your team involved in the community. Offer to volunteer or help a local charity on behalf of your employer. This is a great way to stand out and get noticed.

"When someone tells me something can't be done, I'm ready to go!"

– Hal Wing

The Utah Jazz bear entertaining fans during halftime using a special ladder made for him by Little Giant Ladders. (2018)

CHAPTER FOURTEEN
Building a Life of Legacy

In a world filled with limitations and noes Hal was a "yes" man. Not only did he serve his family, his employees, his business associates and his church, but he also served his community and local businesses. Hal believed in providing value and sharing his gifts whenever the opportunity presented itself. To my dad, there was no such thing as a coincidence. He capitalized on every opportunity to be of service that he could.

Hal loved sports and had season tickets to Utah Jazz basketball games. As I mentioned earlier, my father did not hang out with CEOs and millionaires. He much preferred the company of his employees. Often, he would take them to games and run to the concession stand at breaks to buy all kinds of food and drinks for the group.

The mascot of the Utah Jazz was quite the acrobat, so Hal decided to have some custom ladders made for him to climb during the game breaks. The ladders we built for them were incredibly tall, and they were thrilled to have them. It became the highlight of the game for the mascot to bring out a ladder, climb all the way to the top, then do a handstand on the very top platform. He even did them one-handed, balancing high in the air on the top of a Little Giant Ladder. The crowd went crazy every time, and my dad loved it.

Greg Miller, the former owner of the Utah Jazz, got to know my dad well. "Hal had a heart to serve," Greg recalls. "One time, when we went to a Utah Fast Pass charity event together, Hal was so moved by the cause, he donated his beloved old Porsche…that he had driven to the event. Now there were only a few of these cars in the world, and Hal had said he would never sell it. That night, though, Hal just turned over the keys and told them to use the car to raise more money."

Tom Mabey was in charge of that gala and remembers the evening vividly. "It was right before the live auction was to start. Hal came over to the table and said to me, "I want to give you my car to use in the auction." "Hal was willing to give up a prized possession to help a cause he cared about and knew would help others," said Tom.

Greg and his family bid on the car in the auction and won the bid. "I paid for the car and gave the keys back to Hal. It was a win-win-win that night for sure," he said. Greg also remembers Hal giving away other things like dirt bikes. "Hal once gave me a KTM 450," Greg said. "To this day, I still think of Hal every time I go into my garage and see it. I'll never sell it. Hal was just genuinely nice to everyone and was compelled to share what he had."

Hal made it a point to get involved in other organizations that could reach and help many at a time. One of these was Utah Valley University (UVU). Matt Holland, former president of the university, worked with Hal directly on a number of different projects over the years. "Hal was a great partner. He was a straight shooter, and he had great insight," said Matt. "He knew what he wanted to accomplish, and he knew he could not achieve his goals without people."

Hal was incredibly supportive of the university, and he encouraged big thinking. He spoke at many events and was engaged in helping to develop the vision for the future of the school. When he saw an opportunity to help, he ran right towards it.

My dad was a runner and had actually run marathons when he was in Germany. He never forgot his days as the underdog, and it compelled him to focus his time and attention on others in the same situation. So, he decided to build a track and field facility at UVU because he said, "Runners are athletes, too, and they never get the funding or the attention that football or basketball gets. I want to build a place that celebrates those athletes and gives them the same state-of -the-art equipment and facilities that the more popular sports have." Today, that facility is named the Hal Wing Track and Field.

Because Hal understood the value of hard work and knew that finances could often be a barrier to achievement, he helped individual students as well. Hal partnered with American Indian Services to provide college scholarships for Native American students.

Of course, Hal's love for all things fast influenced his involvement and support. Todd Johnson, a former Little Giant employee who became a Utah Highway Patrolman, remembers his first meeting with Hal. "He came yodeling through the shop as I was working a saw," Todd remembers fondly." At UHP, Todd became the point person for the Utah Fast Pass.

The Fast Pass was a charity fundraising event that focused on performance cars. Each day of the event, the UHP would lead a group through some of Utah's most scenic and thrilling mountain highways. On the third day, the troopers would shut down a 13-mile section and let participants experience the appropriate potential of their cars.

For added fun, participants could choose to run at top speed through a charity radar trap in which the driver's top speed was memorialized with a speeding ticket (suitable for framing), but not memorialized on your driving record, for a tax-deductible donation to one of the designated charities (such as the Utah Highway Patrol's Honoring Heroes Foundation) for whatever the speeding ticket would have been at that speed. Fast cars and charity. As you can imagine, this event had Hal Wing's name all over it. As you read earlier about his Porsche donation, Hal was a huge supporter of and participant in this event.

Tom and Shauna Mabey were former board members of the Utah Fast Pass. "Hal had so much energy," recalls Shauna. "I remember one day of the event, we were at Moab and there were dirt roads, and before breakfast, Hal was out cleaning all the troopers' windshields."

"Hal's generosity was amazing," added Shauna. "Hal's heart was touched, and he touched many hearts. To see someone give in the way Hal did is a life-changing experience. It changed the entire way I look at how I want my life to be in terms of giving back. It has impacted me for the rest of my life."

Hal believed that everyone is welcome. Everyone is deserving. No one is more important than anyone else. He taught that through his actions.

My dad had great admiration for the work of the police and supported their many programs. When Todd came to Hal and asked him for $10,000 for a trooper recognition program, Hal gave him $20,000.

Hal donated two Harley motorcycles to the local police force, and he bought the department their first D.A.R.E. car.

Today, I carry on my father's support of the UHP by sponsoring the annual Hal Wing Memorial Ride. UHP members, motorcycle and car enthusiasts come from multiple states to ride in the event and raise money for the Honoring Heroes Foundation. Thousands of us ride that day in honor of Hal and to support the UHP. It is an event I am proud to support and be a part of each year.

Ever the competitor, Hal always found a way to be in the mix. When the city basketball league needed a win boost, Hal stepped in. Todd Johnson played in the league and remembers that Hal put $200 in a pot. If they won each game, he left the money there. If they lost, he took $100 out. They won every game after that, and at the end of the season, the players all split the money.

My dad donated the land for a beautiful city park in Springville, complete with green space and playground equipment. His only request was that the park be named after his father. Hence, the Ray Arthur Wing City Park was created. Every time I drive by that park and see the name of it, I can't help but think about my dad and grandfather.

The Ray Arthur Wing city park in Springville, Utah was
named after my grandfather (2019)

Hal's generosity often reached far beyond his beloved Springville. Tom Maby recalls one day he was on the phone with Hal. He had just picked up his new Porsche that he had been waiting months for and was on his way to the church office in Salt Lake City. "Hal had heard about the Tsunami and all of the devastation in Thailand, so he drove that car directly to the church office, handed them the keys and told them to sell it and donate the money to help the victims."

"You can do more good with this car than I can," Hal told the church officers. The proceeds from that car no doubt helped many people victimized by that tsunami.

There was no situation or issue that my dad would not tackle head on. There was no amount of time, care or resources that was too big for Hal to step up and help. Those of us around him, and even those who never knew him were better because of it.

Halways:

- Hal was a contributor. In everything he did, he looked for ways to get involved or help.
- No matter what situation presented itself, Hal dealt with it head on.
- Hal was a visionary and a big thinker. It was because he looked several moves ahead that he could see great results.

Hal How-Tos:

How willing are you to give what you have to help or make a difference? Look for a cause you can support, or even just conduct a random act of kindness and buy someone behind you lunch.

Think about your gifts and talents. What are you good at and where do you excel? Take those skills and apply them where they can make a noticeable difference to a non-profit or to people in need. Engaging and getting involved can lead to great things, both in your career and in life.

I have often heard it said that your net worth is directly tied to your network. If that is the case, look for people in your current company that can mentor you. Offer to help them with a project, offer to spend your day off shadowing them, or submit an idea that could cut costs or increase revenue. Relationships are incredibly important when building your career.

"When you climb up a ladder, you must begin at the bottom and ascend step by step, until you arrive at the top."

— Joseph Smith

Me in the "blue room" at Little Giant Ladders corporate offices in Springville, Utah. This photo was used in my retirement announcement in the local press. (2019)

Chapter Fifteen
Ladders I Have Climbed

Knowing how amazing my dad was and hearing it from everyone as I prepared to write this book has been a blessing and a challenge. How can I, as his son, walk in the shadow of such a great man and find my own path to greatness? How can I, through the story of Hal's life, help you find yours?

While I had the benefit of growing up with one of the greatest business minds and American success stories of all time, I also grew up with a great father. My father taught me the value of hard work, discipline, generosity, faith, commitment and integrity.

Growing up, my dad would tell us,

"Because your last name is Wing, you have to work extra hard to prove yourself."

This hit me literally like a slap in the face the first time I asked my dad for a raise. I was young, newly married and working hard at Little Giant, but I needed to make more money so I could buy a house. So, I walked into my dad's office and asked him for a raise to which he promptly replied no. He said to me pointedly, "Son, you are not worth any more to me right now than I am paying you." My dad made sure that we knew we had to earn our place and our money. While it was hard to hear then, I appreciate it now.

Growing up in the Wing household, one thing we never were permitted to have in our home was a sense of entitlement.

Whether it was working on the farm, serving at the church, volunteering in the community, or working at Little Giant cleaning the bathrooms, I always understood from a very young age what it meant to live a life of purpose. Whether I knew it or not at the time, my dad was not only training us to be successful, he was training us to be good citizens.

That also meant being honest and doing the right thing. I can remember it was shortly after my 16th birthday, and my dad and I went motorcycle riding in the desert. I was so excited to have my driver's license. We had a great time together.

On the way back home, my father was speeding…as he often did. He was always in a hurry no matter where he was going. We were driving a Ford Bronco with an enclosed trailer. As we crested a hill of the two-lane road we were on, we passed a county sheriff. My dad looked in his mirror and saw the sheriff slam on his brakes and turn around. My dad quickly pulled over and said to me, "Trade places with me now." The Bronco had a bench seat. My father told me he would surely lose his license if he received one more speeding ticket. It took the sheriff just a few minutes to catch up to us and pull behind us. By the time he came to the window, I was in the driver's seat. I rolled down my window, and the sheriff asked me if I knew how fast I was going. I said I didn't. He told me how fast I was going, and asked for my registration and driver's license.

After the sheriff left, my dad got back in the driver's seat, and we went home. The next morning, my father came down to my room and told me that what he had done was wrong. He asked me to get ready and told me that we were going to go to the home of the Justice of the Peace, and tell him the truth. I was scared. I was sure we would both go to jail. He told me that everything would work out okay, and that we should go and tell the truth.

When we arrived at the home of the Justice of the Peace, my dad introduced us and told him what had happened. I watched the man as my father explained to him that he had a lead foot and that he had been speeding and that we had traded places. After Hal finished his excellent sales presentation, the judge leaned back in his chair and said, "I think everyone here has learned a valuable lesson. Let's just forget this whole thing." That day I was reminded by my father that honesty is definitely always the best policy.

I have so many of these stories filled with laughter, love, generosity, compassion, and of course, adrenaline. Hal was a giant presence, and I am so glad I got to be his son.

Today, I consider myself the steward of Hal Wing's legacy. The leadership, the perseverance, the intuitiveness, the philanthropy...even the need for speed and the "go all out" mentality lives on today in so many ways in our church, our community, at Little Giant, and in me.

As vice-chairman and co-owner, I had the honor of being part of the team that continued to build on the foundation upon which Hal built The Little Giant Ladder company and growing

Me building ladders at the American Fork,
Utah location at 14 years old (1978)

that company to the worldwide powerhouse brand it is today. We were able to expand and grow the business using the same principles I shared with you earlier in this book. Most of the management team is still helping to lead and run the company as it continues to grow and innovate today.

Now in retirement from Little Giant, I am focused on helping entrepreneurs, businesses, sales professionals and anyone who wants to achieve greater success to do so using the same principles Hal used.

I am proud to be told how much like my dad I am. I consider that the best compliment I could ever receive. Like Hal, I climbed the ladder of success, going from cleaning bathrooms to helping run an international company. Hal gave me and so many others that type of opportunity. We were smart enough to recognize it and take it.

Through this book, I wanted to help you get to know not just the hugely successful Hal Wing who founded and built The Little Giant Ladder Company and grew it from his garage to the most popular and well-known ladder brand in the world; but also the Hal Wing who loved his family, was passionate about his business, dedicated to the people he employed, committed to his faith and his church, and intimately connected to his community and his call to use his gifts to serve others. It is all of these qualities that made Hal the giant success that he was, and they all serve as his legacy today. My hope is that sharing this with you will help guide you in your own journey to greatness.

What I think is the most poignant lesson my dad teaches is that the man is the sum of all of his parts, not just one. Hal loved his family more than anything else. After us, my dad was just as committed to his church and his fast cars and dirt bikes as he was to Little Giant. He pursued business and his passions with great focus and attention. I think we can gain from knowing and putting this into practice.

Is there ever such a thing as balance? I don't know. What I do know is that the words of Hal Wing live on today.

"You can accomplish anything with hard work and belief."

Whether you are in your first job or your tenth job; whether you are 20 years old or 50; developing a startup or tending to a seasoned brand; we all must continually learn to grow. Success is not simply achieved…it is a journey.

When my dad was in the hospital and knew he was going to pass, he checked himself out, went home, put on his best suit and went to the office to address the company. He called a meeting with everyone and said good-bye. That speech not only gave Hal the opportunity to bring his work and life full circle, it gave everyone at Little Giant inspiration. Even in facing his own death, Hal was focused on his people, helping them and encouraging them to carry on. He also showed how much he loved and appreciated them by making sure they knew how important they were to him and to the company. Everyone knew this was the last time they would see Hal, and I don't think there was a dry eye in the house. After he spoke, he checked himself back into the hospital and passed away a few days later surrounded by his loving family.

That is the embodiment of Hal Wing: a passionate entrepreneur, an encouraging mentor, a tireless advocate for the underdog, a compassionate leader, a loving family man, and a giving, caring human being.

What can each of us do to live more like Hal—to be purposeful and stand for something meaningful? How can we take our gifts and talents and use them to realize our full potential while pulling others up with us? What kind of life will we choose to lead? What kind of legacy will we choose to leave behind?

As for me, I aspire to continue to use my experiences and blessings to help bless others in my real estate business, my consulting work, my service to my church and my involvement in my community.

What about you? How can you take these principles and the example of the life Hal Wing lived and take action in your own life? Take steps beginning *today* to become a GIANT success in your career.

But also, don't forget to live a full-circle life—with fulfillment, reward, and a bit of an adrenaline rush.

Two GIANT mentors in my life (Left to right) Ray Arthur
Wing, myself, Hal Wing (1983)

Hand written quote taken from my dads journal

HAL WING QUOTES

- "Faster, faster, faster, until the thrill of speed overcomes the fear of death."

- "Every ladder that goes out that door has my name on it, so they have to be of the highest quality."

- "My employees carry me to the top of the mountain every day."

- "I've upped my performance, now up yours."

- "I was born at night, but not last night."

- "When competitors copy us, it is the greatest form of flattery. When they stop copying us, that is the time that we should be worried."

- "Our competitors know what their products are worth, and so do we."

- "We are off like a dirty shirt."

- "I'm going to fill the room full of uppercuts."

- "Three things influence people in life: greed, sex and greed. Most people get a double dose of greed."

- "Don't lie, don't steal and don't be lazy."

- "You are never a loser until you quit."

- "The harder I work, the luckier I get."

- "Never forget, the products make us all look good."

- "If you concentrate on building the business and not the man, you will not achieve. But if you concentrate on building the man, you achieve both."

- "Figures don't lie, but liars figure."

- "It's colder than a mother-in-law's kiss out here."

- "You can tell the customer anything you want to, as long as it's the truth."

- "If you tell me something can't be done, I'm ready to go."

- "Patience is a waste of time."

- "We're burning daylight."

- "Take your time going, but hurry back."

- "I never started my own business to become rich. I started it so that I could work with my sons."

- "If it's not a good deal for everyone around the table, it's not a good deal."

- "I'm so hungry, I could eat the north end of a south bound skunk."

- "Sometimes we all need a check up from the neck up."

- "This is about as much fun as an all night dentist."

- "When starting a business you must remember three things:
    - o It will take twice as long as you think it will;
    - o It will cost twice as much as you think it will; and
    - o You will only make half as much profit as you think you will."

Little Giant Ladders corporate headquarters in
Springville, Utah (2015)

OPPORTUNITY
By Harold R. Wing

I walked the path, alone it seemed
not another soul in sight
I longed to share my fortune great
make another's burden light

Then there he was, just around the bend
sitting with his hand held out
I wondered why he labored not
he appeared so young and stout

And then I thought, it mattered not
I had so much to share
I reached into my pocket deep
to show how much I cared

My offering he gladly took
his pockets he did fill
But as I wandered down the path
I sensed him wanting still

I returned again to this beggar man
and looked at him once more
Twas true, I had given my wealth
but alas, he still was poor

For twas not riches that he lacked
but a feeling of self worth
Something he could only gain
if he earned his way on earth

I wondered aloud, "What can I do
to help this man distraught?"
As I searched my soul and pondered deep
to my mind came this fresh thought

That which I give and he earns not
makes self esteem sink low
He, myself and all Gods sons
need fields, their seeds to sow

I called to him, "Come follow me
I have something for you to see
It may be strange and new to you
tis called opportunity"

He did not move and looked confused
a frown formed on his brow
Had he never dared to try before
did he have the courage now?

Again I bade him, "Come follow me
there's something you can do
For every man was born to win
this rule applies to you"

With cautious steps he moved ahead
and sighed, "I hope I can…
Maybe someday, somehow, I can change
this beggar into a man"

The way was hard and the hill was steep
his brow was covered with sweat
His body ached and longed for rest
sometimes he paused and wept

But deep inside he came to know
and at last to finally see

The only gift that would not degrade
was opportunity

He labored on and learned a trade
and earned his daily bread
At each day's end, where he once felt shame
grew pride and joy instead

I too felt the joy and a sense of pride
for the efforts he had shown
Not for any labor I'd put forth
for the seeds by him were sown

But I now had found the answers sought
when someone is found in need
To shower him with gifts and wealth
is not the proper deed

The way to truly help one grow
and taste of victory
Is to give him something he can use…
Give him opportunity

Hal Wing 1940 - 2012

www.giantsuccess.com